Presented

Mary Jane Wood - Grama!

By

Gina Huinsler

On the Occasion of

Mertle's Passing

Date

_6-18-09_

MOMENTS OF COMFORT

ENCOURAGING MEDITATIONS
FOR TIMES OF LOSS

Moments
of Comfort

Encouraging Meditations
for Times of Loss

Faye Landrum

BARBOUR
PUBLISHING

Published by Barbour Publishing, Inc., P.O. Box 719, Uhrichsville, Ohio 44683, www.barbourbooks.com

Our mission is to publish and distribute inspirational products offering exceptional value and biblical encouragement to the masses.

ecpa Member of the
Evangelical Christian
Publishers Association

Printed in the United States of America.

Contents

INTRODUCTION

Losing a loved one is a life-shattering experience, and life is never quite the same afterward. I know this first-hand because I lost my husband after forty-two years of marriage. I discovered, however, that my Lord was there with me to help "pick up the pieces" and to give comfort, strength, guidance, and even joy. God is waiting and willing to give His help to you, too.

Sometimes death is sudden; sometimes it is prolonged. My "experience" was the latter. After Bob was diagnosed with bone cancer, God granted him eleven more years of life before calling him home to heaven. He died on his sixty-eighth birthday.

In many ways, this gave me time to prepare for the life I would be living alone. I found, however, there was no preparation for the echoes of an empty house and the realization I was a widow. A few years after Bob's death, at age seventy, I moved from Akron, Ohio, to Columbus, to live near one of my sons and his family. I never could have done it without God's sustaining grace. Regardless of your circumstances or the reason you are alone, His grace is likewise available to you.

These sixty short devotionals encompass the experiences of others as well as myself, and sometimes they include the lessons that nature and the Bible teach us. Hopefully they will uplift you and will give you a brighter start to your day or a comforting finish to your evening. We have a great and wonderful Lord who will help you to "pick up the pieces" and find a fulfilling life.

*Special thanks to those who have granted permission
to tell their stories or quote their writings:*

Helen Mallicoat, in "Our Ever-Present Lord"
Debbie Freeman, in "Roses and Thorns"
Margaret Grant, in "Late Answers"
Janice Brown, in "Our Prayer Partner" and
"The Gourd's Hidden Quality"
The International Board of the Southern Baptist
Association, in "Prayer Support"

1

IT'S OKAY TO CRY

Cast all your anxiety on him because he cares for you.
1 PETER 5:7 NIV

Tears are liquid love. They spring from a broken heart like a ruptured reservoir. Don't try to hold them back. As they wash over your sorrow, they are God's way of releasing the tension and hurt that otherwise might explode within you.

Sometimes tears even come unexpectedly. A pungent memory or an uncertain thought about the future may jar open a crack in their storehouse, and they leak out uncontrollably. This is natural after the loss of a loved one.

But remember that Jesus is with you in your grief. He promised He would never leave us—not in good times nor in bad—and you can tell Him how your heart hurts. He understands. Jesus wept at the tomb of Lazarus even though He knew in advance that He would bring His friend back to life (John 11:35). You, too, may have the certainty of life after death, but that does not erase the pain of the present time.

Usually grief follows an expected pattern to its eventual resolution, but the poignancy and length of each phase depends on the circumstances and personalities of those involved. A sudden, unexpected death has a different impact than a prolonged, anticipated demise. A young person's experiences differ from those of the elderly, but the emotional progression from numbness and shock to final acceptance is similar. There may be varying lengths of anxiety, anger, and sadness, but knowing this is normal can be reassuring. It's okay to cry.

Even the loss of a pet often has this same reaction. My son had a black lab that he loved. When the dog died, he retreated into a cocoon of hurt and sorrow. He didn't want to go anywhere or talk to anybody. He would come home from work and shut himself in the bedroom. He didn't even want to eat anything. Gradually he reconciled to the loss, but the process took several days.

David, in the Bible, had a similar reaction when his infant son was mortally ill. He refused to eat, and he spent the night lying on the ground (2 Samuel 12:16–17). Sorrow is a part of life.

It's okay to cry.

*Dear Jesus, please help my tears wash away
the hurt I am feeling. I am so thankful You
love me and understand my grief.*

~

*Pain and pleasure,
light and darkness,
succeed each other.*
LAURENCE STERNE

2

EVERYONE IS DIFFERENT

Don't criticize, and then you won't be criticized.
MATTHEW 7:1 TLB

No two people are the same. Sometimes we fail to realize, however, that we may all react differently to the same circumstances. I found this true in my own family after my husband died.

My younger son has always had a tendency to brood about things, to internalize hurtful situations and withdraw into a response of silence. He was with me during the last days of his dad's illness, and he was at the bedside when God called his dad home to heaven.

My older son has always been more gregarious and more accepting of the hurts that life sometimes throws at him. After his dad died, he and his wife and their three children came from a distant state to be with us for the funeral. Cousins whom they hadn't seen for several years also came from remote areas. They were happy to see each other again, and yes, they laughed about some of the fun they had shared in the past. My younger son could not understand their frivolity, and he communicated his displeasure with a wall of silence the others resented. Both sons were deeply hurt, but their responses were entirely different.

Maybe you have found this to be true with your

family members or friends. The hurt they are feeling and the love and concern they have for you may be equally deep and real, but their ways of expressing them may vary greatly. Some may try to raise your spirits by trivial chatter. Others may seem withdrawn and uncaring because they feel uncertain what they should say in the face of sorrow. It helps to look beneath the surface and understand their motivations.

Likewise, friends or family members may have difficulty understanding your response to them, your desire to be alone, or your readiness to break into tears. To paraphrase an Indian proverb, "Don't criticize others till you walk in their moccasins."

We can be heartened by the realization, however, that Jesus understands us perfectly. As Hebrews 4:15 (NIV) tells us, "We do not have a high priest who is unable to sympathize with our weaknesses."

Dear Jesus, help me to understand others,
and help them to understand me.

~

Trouble is the sieve through which
we sift our acquaintances.
Those too big to pass through
are our friends.
ARLENE FRANCIS

3

THE LOUD SILENCE

"Be still, and know that I am God."
PSALM 46:10 NIV

An oxymoron is a figure of speech in which opposite or contradictory ideas or terms are combined. A "loud silence" is certainly an oxymoron. But that was how I felt about my home after my husband died. The silence seemed to scream at me.

My daughter-in-law and three grandchildren ages two, four, and eight stayed with me for a week after the funeral to "help get me over the hump." I appreciated their concern and my son's willingness for them to do it, but I am not sure they helped much with the "hump." There were many things I needed to do: see my lawyer, go to Social Security, notify insurance companies, settle bank accounts—and I put everything on hold to be with my family.

Three children with rambunctious energy made me feel that I needed to be a social chairperson. One day we went to a park, and another day we went shopping at a mall. Of course the day came when they finally had to leave to go back home, "hump" or no "hump." And that was when the house became my oxymoron.

I stood on the steps and watched them drive off in their rented car to go to the airport. They had a five-hour flight ahead of them. Then I turned and went back into the silent house. Never before had I felt such oppressive stillness. The sudden reality that I was now a widow seemed overpowering.

The flurry of activity and the support of friends and family during those first hectic days after Bob died acted like a tranquilizer that numbed my feelings. I appreciated the demonstration of their love and the support of their sympathy, but of course it had to be short-lived. People had jobs and other things they needed to return to. Time had come to a halt for me, but it hadn't for the rest of the world. I felt as if I were alone on an island.

You may feel that way, too. Reading the Bible, especially the Psalms, has brought solace to many people. Talking to our Lord in prayer gives assurance of His presence. Perhaps turning on the TV, tuning in to a Christian radio station, or playing inspiring CDs would help. The house isn't as "silent" with an auditory companion. Maybe you could invite a friend to share dinner with you.

And always remember that Jesus is there with you. He has told us He would never leave us (Matthew 28:20).

*Thank You that I can count on You always
being with me. It is such a comfort to know I
will never really be alone.*

~

*He departed from our sight
that we might return to our heart,
and there find Him.
For He departed, and behold,
He is here.*
St. Augustine

4

THE ADJUSTMENT ASPECT

"I am your God. I will strengthen you and help you; I will uphold you with my righteous right hand."
ISAIAH 41:10 NIV

After losing a loved one, some adjustments may be very difficult, but God promises to help us through them.

For anyone who has lost a spouse, sleeping alone can be difficult; the other side of the bed is so cold and vacant. One of my friends purchased an electric blanket and found comfort by heating the empty space. Sometimes "help" isn't limited to conventional support.

Eating alone can be a problem. Automatically you may take two place settings from the cupboard, and then you realize you need only one plate. A friend found solace by placing her husband's picture on the table across from her. Sometimes she would even talk to the picture and explain her plans for the day.

When I was a nurse working at a hospital, one of my patients had a picture of her deceased husband sitting on her bedside stand. At the time I thought it was rather morose. After my husband died, however, I understood her reason for wanting it there.

Your loved one's clothes still hanging in the closet may pierce your heart like a dagger. For some, having them there is a comfort, but for others they keep open a wound that never heals. Donating the clothes to a rescue mission where others could be blessed by using them might be one way of helping you cope. Perhaps a friend could do this for you.

One mother who lost a child preserved her little girl's bedroom untouched for several years. It stood as a constant reminder of the pain that wrenched her heart. We all meet sorrow in our own unique ways, but God's advice to live beyond the past, "looking forward to what lies ahead" (Philippians 3:13 NLT) is helpful. And He will be there each step of the way.

Perhaps the most difficult "adjustment" is when finances dictate you can no longer remain in your home. A friend from church faced this dilemma when her husband died and she was left with no income except Social Security. She accepted her son's offer to live with him and his wife. Cementing together the lives of two generations isn't easy, but she has found it is possible. God has given her the needed sustenance to be happy.

Sometimes well-meaning friends offer advice, but their solutions may not be the best ones for you. The next ten years, or the remainder of your life, may depend on the changes you make now. Important decisions should not be made hurriedly, and they should be undergirded with prayer.

Lord, help me to cope with all the changes I have to make.

~

It is difficulties that show what people are.
EPICURIS

5

WISE DECISIONS

*If any of you lacks wisdom, he should ask God. . .
and it will be given to him.*
JAMES 1:5 NIV

With the many decisions we have to make after losing a loved one, it is great to know that God's infinite wisdom is there to help us.

For women who are left alone, one consideration is safety. I recently had lunch with a friend whose husband had died just a few weeks before. About midway through our conversation, she said, "My children are going together to buy a security system for me as a Christmas gift. I think that will make me feel a lot safer."

To her, this constituted a wise decision. Her home sits on a country road, and her nearest neighbor is more than a hearty yell away. Although she may never be threatened by a burglar or by anyone else who would harm her, a security system will give her a welcome sense of safety.

Perhaps deadbolt locks on your doors would give you a similar feeling of security. Maybe replacing the glass windows in your basement with thick, impenetrable glass block would do the same. When I moved into my new home after my husband died, I had a carpenter barricade the crawl space in the basement with a bolted door. That really wasn't necessary, but psychologically it made me feel safe.

I did several other things that helped me have a sense of safety. One of them was a change in my checking account at the bank. Not only did I change the account to be in my name only, but I had new checks printed with only my initials and my last name on them. By looking at them, no one would know whether I was a man or a woman. I also had my phone number removed from the checks. Approximately sixteen people handle each check on its route through the banking system, and I didn't want anyone to know I was a woman living alone.

"The less strangers know about you, the better it is," my son advised. "You never know what kooks may be out there."

Another safety precaution is a male voice on the phone recorder. I had my son dictate the message: "We cannot come to the phone right now. Please leave your name and number, and we will get back to you as soon as possible."

In the phone category, I retained my husband's name in the phone book listing. Anyone just scanning down the line of numbers would never know I was alone. Of course an unlisted number is obtainable if that safeguard seems judicious.

Security doesn't need to be a fetish, but certainly God intends for us to be prudent in our preparations. And He is there to give us His wisdom when we need it.

Thank You for making Your wisdom
available when I need it.

~

Wisdom is ofttimes nearer when
we stoop than when we soar.
WILLIAM WORDSWORTH

6

TEMPLE CARE

*Don't you know that you yourselves are God's temple
and that God's Spirit lives in you?*
1 CORINTHIANS 3:16 NIV

After losing a loved one, it is so easy to get lost in sorrow and to neglect taking care of God's temple. Or didn't you know that as a Christian, your body is the abiding place of the Holy Spirit—God's temple—and you need to give it the best care possible?

Just as our church's janitor needs to take good care of the building where we worship, we need to take "good care" of the temple where the Holy Spirit lives. Among other things, this means nourishing this "temple" with a healthy diet. Being alone, we tend to forget about eating, lost in our sorrow, or we indulge in easy-to-prepare snacks that act as "comfort foods." A hint that we are neglecting to give proper care to God's temple is either loss of weight or an increase in our girth.

If dining alone inhibits your eating the right foods, maybe you have a grandchild who would welcome an outing to a restaurant. Or maybe you have a friend who would enjoy sharing an occasional dinner with you. Possibly you know an elderly neighbor who would appreciate a luncheon invitation. There is no greater incentive for healthy cooking than sharing meals with someone else.

Remember how Daniel proved the advantages of a healthy diet in the Old Testament? He and his friends requested vegetables and water instead of rich foods and wine, and in ten days they were healthier than their counterparts who ate the royal diet (Daniel 1:8–16). Should we do any less for "God's temple"?

Good care also includes activity; it hones the temple and stimulates the psyche. A muscle that isn't used atrophies, and a body resigned to inactivity becomes flabby. After I lost my husband, I joined a YWCA and went to an exercise class three mornings a week. Maybe you prefer a morning stroll with a neighbor or an outing to a park with a grandchild. Oftentimes malls and churches with activity centers open their doors for early-morning walkers, and this is especially attractive in bad weather.

If you have the space for a garden, pulling weeds is excellent exercise. Also, flowers will help to spruce up your spirits, and veggies can perk up your diet.

Proper rest is also needed to maintain the "temple," and our wonderful, comforting, ever-present Lord can help us realize this, too.

Dear Jesus, help me to take
good care of Your temple.

~

The preservation of health is a duty.
HERBERT SPENCER

7

A Divine Sleep Aid

"Come to me, all you who are weary and burdened, and I will give you rest."
MATTHEW 11:28 NIV

A friend once told me, "When you have trouble sleeping, talk to the Shepherd instead of counting His sheep." After losing a loved one, sleep is sometimes difficult to come by, but rest is so needed to nourish our bodies.

Occasionally just the sounds of the night may keep us awake. Strange how we never noticed the furnace clicking on and off or crickets chirping outside till we were alone in an empty house. It is comforting to know, however, that our Lord doesn't sleep. Psalm 121:3 (NIV) says, "He who watches over you will not slumber." Our Lord is better protection than a watchdog, and with Him "in charge" we can go to sleep.

Sleep may also elude us because we mentally rehearse the problems of the day as soon as we lie down at night. Or perhaps we let our minds churn up reasons why we may be inadequate to handle our future. Troubles always loom greater at night than in the morning. It helps if we give each problem to our Lord—and leave it there. He is going to be awake anyway, and we need the sleep.

First Peter 5:7 (NIV) tells us, "Cast all your anxiety

on him because he cares for you." The secret to a good night's sleep is to leave that "anxiety" with the Lord, after we cast it off to Him. He can handle it.

Sometimes writing about our troubles in a notebook helps the "casting" process. Problems don't seem quite as threatening when we give them substance and can tangibly examine them. Each night I write a letter to Jesus. I thank Him for the blessings of the day, and I tell Him about the complications that may come tomorrow. I always finish my letter by telling Him I love Him. Doing this may not be helpful to you, but it has helped me.

Even our subconscious may give us a restless night. Our defenses are down then, and our fears or regrets may become more poignant. Reading a spiritually uplifting book or magazine or watching a program on the Christian TV channel just before shutting off the light may help. And of course talking to "the Shepherd" or reading His Word is always helpful.

We spend one-third of our lives in bed, and we need to take advantage of the rest that God can give us.

Lord Jesus, thank You for watching over me during the night, and help me to get the rest that I need.

~

Go to sleep in peace.
God is awake.
VICTOR HUGO

8

THE POWER OF FORGIVENESS

*Be kind and compassionate to one another, forgiving
each other, just as in Christ God forgave you.*
EPHESIANS 4:32 NIV

When a specific person has caused the loss of a loved one, the natural response is to hate that person and want revenge and retaliation. But bitterness is like an acid that corrodes the container that holds it, and it destroys the people it spills onto.

As unrealistic as it may at first seem, forgiveness is like opening the blinds in a dark room and letting God's sunshine pervade the premises. The alternative is a bitterness that will fester and grow, robbing joy and causing separation from friends and from God. Our Lord gives us the choice, assuring us that His grace is sufficient for our every need (2 Corinthians 12:9).

Corrie ten Boom discovered that God's grace could enable her to forgive the man who had tortured her and her sister in the Nazi concentration camp. After the war, he had become a Christian, and he was in the audience when she was giving a speech about her experiences. He came to her afterward and asked for her forgiveness. At first she didn't think she could do it, but she knew well the admonition of Matthew 6:15 (NIV): "If you do not forgive men their sins, your Father will not forgive your sins."

As an act of the will, she mechanically extended her hand toward the guard, praying that Jesus would give her the emotion she needed for forgiveness, and He did. When she took the man's hand, a current seemed to pass from her shoulder, along her arm, and through her hand to his. An incredible love for this stranger almost overwhelmed her.

In 1948, during an initiation into the Corps of Cadets, a military-style training program at A&M University, upperclassmen forced incoming students to run several miles in hot, humid conditions. As a result of this harassment, one young man collapsed and died. His father grieved greatly, but he later wrote a letter to the administration and told them he harbored no ill will. He said he could do this because he knew his son was now secure in his celestial home, and he hoped it would cause others to seriously consider where they will spend eternity.

People were amazed at his ability to forgive those who caused the tragedy. Forgiveness is not easy, but with God's help it is possible.

As Corrie ten Boom later discovered, however, forgiveness is something that has to be executed each new time the need for it confronts our minds. Unlike God, who forgives our sins once and forever, our human psyche needs reinforcement. But our forgiveness unleashes God's joy.

Lord, help me to forgive others
as You have forgiven me.

Forgiveness is like faith.
You have to keep reviving it.
MASON COOLEY

9

Thought Control

Your attitude should be the same
as that of Christ Jesus.
Philippians 2:5 NIV

Envy slips in so easily after we lose a loved one. For a woman who has lost a husband, just seeing happy couples together at church may evoke a pained response. She may think, *I wish I still had my husband.* A more subtle assault may come when she drives by a home at night and a lighted window shows a couple sharing their evening meal. Remembering how life used to be when she shared meals with her loved one may give her pangs of jealousy.

If a couple has lost a child, seeing children at play in a schoolyard may likewise make them envious. When seeing a wedding picture in a newspaper, they realize they will never see their child in such a picture, and they wish so much that they could.

So how do we handle these emotions? Like all trauma that attacks us after losing a loved one, we need to turn it over to Jesus.

In 1896 a Christian novelist, Charles Sheldon, wrote a book titled *In His Steps.* It was a thinly veiled story about real social problems facing the populace of Topeka, Kansas. The book explored the possible consequences of people continually asking themselves, "What would

Jesus do?" The novel had a great influence in Topeka. A local newspaper actually adopted W.W.J.D. (What Would Jesus Do) as an editorial policy for a month.

More than a hundred years later a youth group in Holland, Michigan, studied Sheldon's book, and the modern W.W.J.D. phenomenon was born. The movement spread rapidly, and commercialism fanned its increase like a Santa Ana wind spreading a brush fire. T-shirts, bracelets, CDs, album covers, and posters sprang up overnight.

The youth especially embraced it. It became a handy slogan that mimicked legalism: Do this, wear that, sit like this, etc. It assumed that Christians are able to correctly deduce what Jesus would do in a given situation, but it became a matter of personal interpretation. The Bible gives no hint of what Jesus "would do." It tells what He did do.

A better slogan to follow is W.D.J.D. What Did Jesus Do? How did He treat His disciples and His followers? How did He show love to children? How did He react to controversy? And yes, how did He treat people who were envious or jealous (see Luke 15:11–31)?

The Bible tells us we should have the same attitude as Jesus (Philippians 2:5), and our Lord will help us do it.

Dear Jesus, I so often wish I had my loved one back with me. Help me not to be envious of those who still have theirs.

~

Let the matchless love of God sweep away your doubts and fears. You already have God's attention and you will never lose it.
Joni Eareckson Tada

10

THE "WHAT IF" COMPLEX

*Take captive every thought to make it
obedient to Christ.*
2 CORINTHIANS 10:5 NIV

When we lose a loved one, forgiving ourselves is sometimes more difficult than forgiving others—particularly if we somewhat blame ourselves for the death. The "what if" complex goes something like this: *What if I had stayed home instead of going to the civic meeting, would he have died? If I had called 911 sooner, would it have made any difference?* The possibility of manufactured "what ifs" can go on and on, and the more we rehearse them, the more foreboding they become.

A couple in our church faced this oppression. A young mother left to go to the store for a loaf of bread and a quart of milk while her husband stayed home to babysit. Her two sons, ages three and five, were playing with a ball on the front lawn. As she started to back out of the garage, the ball bounced behind the car and her three-year-old came running after it. She stomped on the brake, but it was too late. The tires ran over her baby and killed him.

Guilt and sorrow devastated her, and the "what ifs" played like a broken record in her subconscious. *What if I had backed out more slowly? What if I had paid more attention to what the kids were doing? What if I had gone to the store yesterday instead of playing tennis?* The more she condemned herself, the deeper the "what ifs" bored into her mind.

So what is the solution? As always, God's Word has an answer for us. Romans 8:1 (NIV) says, "There is now no condemnation for those who are in Christ Jesus." Accidents and mistakes happen to us all. If God doesn't condemn us, we should not condemn ourselves.

But what do we do with the persistent "what if" that plagues us? Our minds can handle only one thought at a time, and focusing on Jesus pushes our "what ifs" to the periphery. It takes practice, but it pays worthwhile dividends. Devour God's Word (instead of giving it a superficial reading), pray fervently, attend church, and focus on the needs of others. Reading spiritual books and listening to Christian CDs or radio will help. Talking with a friend, pastor, or counselor may be beneficial. Certainly God does not want us crippled by oppression from our past.

Jesus said, "In this world you will have trouble. But take heart! I have overcome the world" (John 16:33 NIV). As we give our problems to Jesus, He helps us "overcome" the pain.

*Lord Jesus, help me not to
focus on the "what ifs."*

*He is always moving about His work
to shape and arrange events
in His wise government of our lives.*
JOHN OF THE CROSS

11

WHEN TRUST ISN'T EASY

It is better to trust in the Lord
than to put confidence in man.
Psalm 118:8 KJV

Trusting God is sometimes not easy—especially if He has not answered one of your prayers in the way you wanted. Perhaps you feel He didn't grant your most urgent plea when He allowed your loved one to die. But trust is not a matter of eyesight; it is a matter of faith.

We have the Bible's assurance that when we talk to God in prayer, He hears us (1 John 5:14–15). Those verses also say He will grant our petitions, but those "petitions" are filtered to give us what is best, not necessarily what we have in mind. Sometimes, like a small child who has to wait many years to acknowledge that his father's occasional refusal to let him have his own way was for his benefit, we have to wait for hindsight to know that what He did was really best.

In ancient times, Joseph must have felt God didn't answer his prayer "for his benefit" when his jealous brothers threw him into an abandoned well. The Bible doesn't tell us he prayed, but judging from his character, I am sure he did. Many years later, when he was second in charge of all Egypt, he said to his brothers, "You intended to harm me, but God intended it for good to accomplish what is now being done, the saving of many lives" (Genesis 50:20 NIV).

Job went as far as to say, "Though he slay me, yet will I trust in him" (Job 13:15 KJV).

Perhaps you have read the prayer that was found on the body of an unknown Confederate soldier. We don't know his name or any of the circumstances of his life, but we know he discovered the trustworthiness of God.

> *I asked God for strength that I might achieve;*
> > *I was made weak, that I might learn humbly to obey.*
> *I asked for health, that I might do greater things;*
> > *I was given infirmity that I might do better things.*
> *I asked for riches, that I might be happy;*
> > *I was given poverty, that I might be wise.*
> *I asked for power, that I might have the praise of men;*
> > *I was given weakness, that I might feel the need of God.*
> *I asked for all things, that I might enjoy life;*
> > *I was given life, that I might enjoy all things.*
> *I got nothing that I asked for—*
> > *but everything I had hoped for.*
> *Almost despite myself, my unspoken prayers were answered.*
> *I am, among all men, most richly blessed.*

If trust were easy, it wouldn't be trust; it would be observance. Don't be afraid to trust our loving God.

Lord, please help me to trust You
even when I don't feel like doing it.

~

When we face the worst that can happen
in any situation, we grow.
When circumstances are at their worst,
we can find our best.
ELIZABETH KÜBLER ROSS AND DAVID KESSLER

12

OUR LIVING SAVIOR

*"I am the Living One; I was dead,
and behold I am alive for ever and ever!"*
REVELATION 1:18 NIV

When my husband was terminally ill with cancer, we both knew that his time to remain on earth was very short. I felt panic stricken when I thought of losing him and being left alone. As a born-again Christian, he knew where he was going—but I was going to be left with all the problems.

I didn't know how to start the lawnmower or run the snowblower. I didn't know how to change the oil in the car. He always took care of those things. I did the cooking and managed the inside of the house. I thought I did well to know how to change a lightbulb.

One night when we went to bed I was silently stewing about my inadequacies and fearing I could never cope. In the middle of the night the words of a song by Bill Gaither, "Because He Lives," played out in my subconscious. I began to realize that I could face the next day, my fear gone, because God held the future. Life was worth living.

The words still resonated in my mind when morning came. True, I probably remembered the song because we had recently sung it at church, but it seemed like a personal message to me from our Lord. We have a *living* Savior—not a dead prophet somewhere in a grave. He is *living*! He is living, and He is with me now. And He will be with me in the future when I need Him.

The knowledge of His presence made such a difference to me. With Him, I could face life—with or without my husband. I printed out the words to the song and posted them at the desk where I made phone calls and wrote out checks to pay bills. Whenever I began to be afraid, I would read those words and be comforted with the reassurance that we have a *living* Savior, and He is with me.

After my husband went home to be with the Lord in heaven, those same words comforted me and empowered me. With God's presence, I knew I could somehow handle the challenges that life would throw at me. And I did.

This same Lord, our *living* Savior, is with you, too. He is only a prayer away.

Thank You, Jesus, for being our living Savior.

*God came to us because God wanted
to join us on the road, to listen to our story,
and to help us realize that we are
not walking in circles but
moving toward the house of peace and joy.*
THOMAS MERTON

13

OUR EVER-PRESENT LORD

[Jesus said,] "And surely I am with you always,
to the very end of the age.
MATTHEW 28:20 NIV

Just as I discovered that Jesus is our *living* Savior, Helen Mallicoat did—but in a different way. One night when she was dozing, words to a poem formed in her mind. The poem came to her in its entirety, and she wrote it down. To anyone who asks her about it, she always replies, "The words are not mine. They are the Lord's words to His precious children."

The poem's title assures us that God is an ever-abiding presence:

MY NAME IS "I AM"
I was regretting the past
and fearing the future.
Suddenly my Lord was speaking:
"MY NAME IS 'I AM.' "
I waited, God continued:
"When you live in the past,
with its mistakes and regrets,
it is hard. I am not there.
"MY NAME IS NOT 'I WAS.' "
When you live in the future,
with its problems and fears,

it is hard. I am not there.
    "MY NAME IS NOT 'I WILL BE.' "
When you live in this moment,
it is not hard. I am here.
    "MY NAME IS 'I AM.' "

"I AM" is the present tense. Why should we worry about the future? When "the future" becomes the "present time," our Lord is right there with us—and nothing is too great for Him to handle.

When Moses was commissioned by the Lord to go to Pharaoh in Egypt and demand the release of the Israelites, he, too, discovered that God's name is "I AM." Standing by the burning bush that fire didn't consume, Moses expressed skepticism. "Suppose I go to the Israelites and say to them, 'The God of your fathers has sent me to you,' and they ask me, 'What is his name?' Then what shall I tell them?"

God replied, "I AM WHO I AM. This is what you are to say to the Israelites: 'I AM has sent me to you'" (Exodus 3:13–14 NIV).

When the Jews scoffed at Jesus because He indicated Abraham had seen Him, Jesus replied, "I tell you the truth. . .before Abraham was born, I am!" (John 8:57–58 NIV).

God's name of "I AM" is a precious assurance of His ever-abiding presence with us. That is why Helen Mallicoat's poem has meant so much to so many. For more than thirty years, it has been an encouragement and a great blessing to millions of people. It has been published in *Guideposts*, *Angel Awareness*, *A Brighter Day*, *Harvester—Gospel Tract Society*, and many more. I quoted it in the book I wrote, *The Final Mile*, about the last six months of my husband's battle with bone cancer. That poem was a great comfort to me during those last six months and in my life alone afterward.

I pray it will also be a blessing and an encouragement to you.

Dear Jesus, I am so thankful
Your name is "I AM."

~

Have confidence in God's mercy,
for when you think
He is a long way from you,
He is often quite near.
THOMAS Á KEMPIS

14

Our Prayer Partner

*We don't even know what we should pray for,
nor how to pray as we should, but the Holy Spirit
prays for us with such feeling that it cannot
be expressed in words.*
Romans 8:26 TLB

My son is a corporate pilot, and sometimes he has to fly in stormy weather. Thick clouds may form a dense canopy above him. A heavy rain may pelt the plane's fuselage, and visibility may be so poor he has to rely on his instruments for flying. His radio, however, keeps him in contact with the control tower.

There may be days when our grief is so oppressive that we, too, feel locked in by thick storm clouds or a dense, impenetrable fog. We may even feel as if life has become so meaningless that we are "flying by instruments." And God seems unreachable.

That is when we need to realize that the Holy Spirit keeps us in contact with our "Control Tower." When we don't know what to pray for, or how to pray, He prays for us "with such feeling that it cannot be expressed in words."

One of my friends learned that her father had just been diagnosed with lymphoma. The doctor said there was no cure for this cancer. In an e-mail to me she said, "You can understand when I say I am numb. Praying is hard when your body feels nothing, but I know God understands and hears my heart. He is certainly sheltering us through this storm."

God knows our hearts. And He knows "what the Spirit is saying as he pleads for us in harmony with God's own will" (Romans 8:27 TLB). What a privilege it is to have such a prayer partner.

When my son's plane climbs to an altitude of thirty thousand feet, it may break through the clouds and be embraced by warm sunshine. The clouds are still there, but now they are beneath him. Blue skies envelop him—and his radio keeps him in contact with the control tower.

Our Lord invites us to bring our fears, our worries, and our hopes to Him in prayer. Just as an earthly father wants to communicate and comfort his children, our heavenly Father also wants us to talk to Him and share our problems and requests. Even if we are so distraught we don't know what to say, we can be certain the Holy Spirit—our Prayer Partner—will decode our "message" according to God's will. And He will help to lift us above the "clouds" to bask in the warmth of God's "sunshine."

Thank You for giving me Yourself as a prayer partner.

~

*The wings of prayer
can carry high and far.*
ANONYMOUS

15

PRAYER SUPPORT

*The prayer of a righteous man
is powerful and effective.*
JAMES 5:16 NIV

Matt and Lora Higgins, missionaries in Africa, were leaving to go back to the United States for a much-deserved furlough. They were driving through Mau Mau country on their way to the coast when their Land Rover's engine sputtered and died. Matt looked under the hood to determine the problem, but he couldn't find the reason for the trouble.

As night started to envelop them, Matt knew he would never have enough light to fix the trouble, even if he could find it. They were seventeen miles from the city of Nairobi, and with no phone or means of communication, they decided they would have to spend the night in a place they knew was extremely dangerous.

White men had been brutally murdered in that area. Christian natives had also lost their lives. When one of them had disappeared during the night, the next morning the missionaries found the man's body scattered in pieces over the hillside. Once an African took the dreadful oath of a Mau Mau, he became an unscrupulous thief and killer.

The next morning Matt finally diagnosed the trouble with the Land Rover's engine and repaired it.

They arrived in Nairobi by midmorning. Later when a native pastor visited them, he said, "I have found out something I think you will want to hear. When you had to spend the night in your car, four Mau Maus crept up on you, intending not only to rob you but to murder you. They didn't carry out their plans because they were afraid of the sixteen men surrounding your Land Rover."

The young couple stared at the native pastor incredulously. "Sixteen men! We don't know what you're talking about."

The mystery of the sixteen men wasn't resolved till the missionaries were back in the United States. Besides enjoying rest and relaxation with friends and relatives, their lives were filled with traveling— preaching and showing slides of Africa in an effort to challenge others to go to the Dark Continent.

At one of the meetings, an old-time friend approached Matt. After they chatted for a while, his friend asked him if ever there was a time he had been in great danger. Matt told him about the harrowing night of March 23 that he and Lora had spent in Mau Mau country.

"On that same day," his friend said, "the Lord laid a burden on my heart for you. It was so heavy that I called some of the men, and we met here at the church and prayed until the burden lifted. There were sixteen of us."

If you, too, have a burden, don't hesitate to share it with those who will pray for you.

Thank You, Lord, for hearing the prayers of
those who pray for us.

~

Pray for my soul.
More things are wrought by prayer
than this world dreams of.
ALFRED LORD TENNYSON

16

LITTLE THINGS MATTER

*In everything, by prayer and petition. . .
present your requests to God.*
PHILIPPIANS 4:6 NIV

Is our Lord interested in the "little things" that provoke our lives? His Word tells us that He is. He invites us to bring *everything* to Him in prayer.

Sometimes the best way to lessen the sting of a recurring memory is to change the thing that evokes it, and our Lord can help us do it. Perhaps there is a recliner that was your husband's favorite chair when he watched the evening news, and every time you pass by it, you want to cry. Perhaps moving it to a different part of the room would diminish the hurt. Or possibly a slipcover that would change its appearance would help. Maybe just replacing it with a new chair would be the most beneficial change. Don't feel it is too small a problem for divine consideration; our God wants to help.

Possibly a change in your own appearance would lift your spirits: a new hairstyle, new clothes, different jewelry. The boredom that free time introduces might be counteracted by a new hobby or a new outreach. One of my friends took up quilting after the loss of her loved one. Another friend learned to play the piano.

Grief has stages of progression that need to be

addressed, but gradually adjusting one's life to new circumstances is part of the healing process. And our Lord wants to give help with each small step. No problem or change is too insignificant for His attention.

Soon after my husband died, friends gave me an amaryllis plant that grew thirty-five inches tall and produced six bright red blooms. It towered above an adjacent coffeepot that was guarded by a tiny half-inch ceramic dog I had named Frisky. My husband had given it to me, and I adored it. The plant was gorgeous, but it was top-heavy. One day it bent in half and toppled over, and the next day I couldn't find Frisky anywhere. To me Frisky was an important cog in my memory collection, and I prayed about finding it. Finally I decided it must have been swept away when I cleaned up the debris from the crumpled flower, and I searched through a week's worth of trash and garbage. I was about to give up when I found Frisky at the bottom of the white plastic trash bag.

Yes, our wonderful Lord is interested in even the "little things" in our lives. If He is concerned about anything as trivial as a half-inch ceramic dog, He certainly cares about the other problems that trouble us.

Lord Jesus, thank You that I can
talk to You about everything.

~

When we take time to notice
the simple things in life,
we never lack for encouragement.
We discover that we are surrounded
by limitless hope
that's just wearing everyday clothes.
ANONYMOUS

17

ONE DAY AT A TIME

Your strength will equal your days.
DEUTERONOMY 33:25 NIV

One evening heavy rain with high winds severed several branches from the sassafras trees that shaded my backyard. The next morning I saw the debris when I looked out my window. Alone since my husband's death, I moaned, as the task of cleaning up the yard seemed insurmountable.

"How will I ever get this mess cleaned up?" I said half-aloud.

I dialed my neighbor's phone number to ask if their teenage son could give me a hand. He had used a saw to cut up some downed branches for me after a previous storm, and I was hoping he could lend muscle power to this predicament, too. The phone rang several times, but there was no answer. Then I remembered that the family was away for the week on vacation.

"I guess it's up to You and me, Lord," I said as I headed to the shed to gather some tools. I had no idea how I was going to clear away the rubble, and I prayed for divine strength to help me.

The first limb I approached was about six feet long. I broke off one of the small branches from the main trunk and stuffed it into a trash bag. The ease with which it snapped off surprised me. I moved to another branch and found this one snapped off easily too.

A few minutes later, only the main trunk of the limb remained. I was sure that would be my downfall. To my astonishment, I found when I put my foot on the limb and pulled it upward, it easily snapped in two. The wood of sassafras trees is very brittle in dead branches.

In a little more than an hour, I had the backyard completely cleared of debris. By breaking off the small branches first, then tackling the main trunk, I had easily accomplished the task.

With the work finished, I thanked God for showing me how it should be done. I realized then, this is the same way He shows us how to conquer most of our problems: one branch at a time, one problem at a time, one day at a time. If we nibble away at a problem instead of trying to chew up the whole thing at once, we can usually handle it.

*Lord, please help me try to solve my problems
one day at a time—maybe one hour at a time.*

*Prayer is not conquering God's reluctance,
but taking hold of God's willingness.*
PHILLIPS BROOKS

18

GAINING GOALS

Run in such a way as to get the prize.
1 CORINTHIANS 9:24 NIV

One evening I went with my son and his wife and three-year-old daughter to an adjacent town for an after-dinner ice cream treat. After we came out of the restaurant, we decided to do a little window-shopping. About three stores down the sidewalk, my granddaughter indicated she wanted to be carried. My daughter-in-law obliged, but after a few minutes she handed Janessa over to my son.

Three-year-old granddaughters can become quite heavy. As we turned to go back to our car, my son lowered Janessa to the sidewalk. When she registered some displeasure, he asked, "Do you see that fence down there?" He indicated a picket fence that abutted the sidewalk about fifty feet away.

Janessa said she saw it.

"Do you think you could walk to that fence?"

"Yes."

"Okay, you walk to the fence, then I will carry you."

And off we started again on our return to the car. When we reached the fence, my son gave Janessa another goal to achieve—and she walked all the way to the car.

Have you tried achieving goals? Not big ones, but little ones. The question is asked, "How do you eat an elephant?" The answer is: "One bite at a time." The one-bite theory also holds true for setting goals.

Choose a goal you know you would probably be able to achieve. Do you have laundry that needs to be done? Just one load of laundry isn't too difficult a task. But it is a step in the right direction. One load at a time, and almost before you realize it, you will have a closet full of clean clothes.

Do you have letters that need to be written? You could probably handle writing one letter today. Just one. Put the others away, and don't think about them. You can praise God you have accomplished your intended goal—and tomorrow you can write one more letter.

The apostle Paul likened life to running a race, and his advice was to run in such a way as to "get the prize" (1 Corinthians 9:24). Of course he wasn't talking about writing letters or washing clothes, but the principle is the same. With God's help, you can accomplish your goals, one at a time, and the achievement is exhilarating. It can act as an antidote to your grief.

Lord, help me to achieve some goals—
one at a time.

God grant me the serenity to
accept the things I cannot change,
courage to change the things I can,
and the wisdom to know the difference.
REINHOLD NIEBUHR

19

A Heavenly Husband

The sorrows of widowhood will be remembered no more, for your Creator will be your "husband."
Isaiah 54:4–5 TLB

The dictionary describes a husband as the manager of a household. When I was left alone, I found comfort in knowing that God was now my "husband," and He would help me "manage my household." I think He has a special concern for widows—for those who are left alone, for whatever reason.

After an especially rainy summer, hardy weeds usurped my garden and the landscaping next to the house. I devoted several days to pulling weeds and trimming shrubs. My dedicated effort resulted in filling up four trash bags with refuse. In the town where I live, such "refuse" has to be placed in large, recyclable paper bags and brought to the side of the road.

The evening before trash was to be collected the next morning, I began the difficult task of moving the bags from the garage to the end of my driveway. They were heavy, and there was no way I could pick them up. My only way of advancing them toward the road was an improvised shoe lift. By putting one foot under the bag and kicking it forward, I could laboriously advance it toward my destination.

I remember thinking, *I sure wish there was someone*

who could help me. It wasn't a prayer, just a passing wish, but a few minutes later a car stopped and a young man asked, "Would you like some help?"

"I sure would," I responded.

He was a handsome young man, probably in his early twenties. He picked up my refuse bag in one hand and whisked it to the curb. When he came back for the next bag, he explained he had been visiting my neighbor across the street.

On his next trek down the driveway, the bottom of the bag started to disintegrate. Wet weeds had caused the heavy paper to fall apart. But this didn't faze him in the least. I gave him a new trash bag, and he funneled my wet weeds into a new home.

I had never seen him before, and I have never seen him since, but he was there when I needed him. After he left, I remembered the verse of Scripture that says, "Before they call I will answer; while they are still speaking I will hear" (Isaiah 65:24 NIV). Even before my "wish" became a prayer, God sent a helper.

Now isn't that just like a "husband"?

*Thank You, Jesus, for knowing
my needs even before I tell You.*

*God may be invisible,
but He's in touch.
We may not be able to see Him,
but He is in control.*
CHARLES SWINDOLL

20

GOD'S SUPPLY LINE

And my God will meet all your needs according to his glorious riches in Christ Jesus.
PHILIPPIANS 4:19 NIV

Often God's provisions are right at hand, and we don't even know they are there. After the loss of a loved one, we are often so involved in looking at the "big picture" that we don't notice the individual pieces that make up the total puzzle.

When I moved into my new home after my husband died, the dining area had an empty wall under a picture; it really did need "something." I decided a teacart would be just perfect in that position. Not only would it occupy the wall, but it could also be pulled up next to the table as a serving counter.

I couldn't find a suitable teacart in any of the stores, and my son suggested I might have one made. He gave me the name of a craftsman who fashioned furniture, and I called him.

"Sure," he said. "I can do it. No problem."

The "problem" was that somehow we had a breakdown in communication. When the craftsman delivered my new teacart, it was not what I had in mind.

I had envisioned a small, mobile cart the height of the dining room table. This cart towered a foot above the table, and its four-foot length and wide breadth did not lend itself to mobility. I really didn't want it crowding the furniture in the dining room.

Now I had the problem of what to do with it. My son suggested putting it in the living room and decorating it with a few books and a bouquet of flowers. Then, as he surveyed the premises, he said, "You could move that stand, or whatever it is, from the sun room to the dining room."

A lightbulb came on in my head. I looked at that "stand" in a way I had never seen it before. It was oak, just like the dining room furniture. The design of its doors even matched the decor of the oak kitchen cabinets. It wasn't a teacart, but it was just what I needed for the empty wall in my dining room.

I had looked at that television stand millions of times and never seen its potential till my son pointed it out to me. And occasionally isn't that the way it is with the Lord's blessings to us? We become so accustomed to His daily benefits to us we don't see them. God has said He would take care of our "needs," but He doesn't tell us how He will do it.

Thank You for taking care of me—often in
ways I don't even realize.

~

A burden, even a small one,
when carried alone
and in isolation, can destroy us,
but a burden when carried as
part of God's burden
can lead us to new life.
That is the great mystery of our faith.
HENRI NOUWEN

21

GOD'S HANDIWORK

O LORD, how manifold are thy works!
in wisdom hast thou made them all:
the earth is full of thy riches.
PSALM 104:24 JKV

Our home faced toward the east, and one morning while I was preparing breakfast, my twelve-year-old son exclaimed, "Oh, Mom, come here. God has been at the easel again."

I went into the living room to look out the window with him. The first rays of sunshine painted the horizon a soft red radiance intermingled with threads of gold. God had indeed painted a beautiful picture.

For over forty years I have remembered my son's excited observation, and I have often wondered how much of our Lord's artwork I have missed seeing. I do remember one morning, after a heavy, wet snowfall the night before, He crafted an especially gorgeous picture. As I drove to work past a grove of evergreen trees, each bough wore a heavy ermine wrap that glowed from the touch of the morning sun.

I have often heard the admonishment, "Don't be so busy that you forget to smell the roses." In the rush of this modern-day society, we often fail to do just that. Do we stop to appreciate the velvety softness of rose petals or to enjoy their delightful fragrance?

Are we thankful for the food that God provides for

us? Seeds possess remarkable properties. A turnip seed, for example, is only about one-twentieth of an inch in diameter, but it enlarges twenty-seven thousand times its original size after a few months' growth.

When we see a butterfly flitting from one flower to another, do we stop to marvel at its function as well as its beauty? Did you know that butterflies taste with their feet? They don't have noses; they smell with their antennae. A butterfly's mouth stays rolled up until it is time to eat, then it acts like a drinking straw, consuming only liquid foods such as nectars from flowers or fruit.

Hummingbirds frequent our bird feeder in the summertime. Each one weighs only two or three grams. It would take five hummingbirds to equal the weight of a chickadee, and each one is only about three inches long. Yet these tiny creatures fly nonstop about five hundred miles to migrate to the Gulf of Mexico each fall and return to the United States in the spring.

Isn't God's craftsmanship amazing? Our grief can take a backseat as we revel in the beauty and wonderment of His "handiwork." And how thrilling it is to realize that He values us more than any of His other creations (Luke 12:24). Only for us did He give His Son to be a ransom for our sins (Matthew 20:28).

Thank You, Jesus, for Your wonderful world.
Help me to be more thankful
for Your provisions.

Any one thing in the creation is sufficient
to demonstrate a Providence
to an humble and grateful mind.
EPICTECUS

22

WINNING THE WORRY WAR

Give your burdens to the Lord. He will carry them.
PSALM 55:22 TLB

Winning the worry war is often one of the most difficult spiritual battles we face after the loss of our loved one. The "tomorrows" loom ahead of us like huge icebergs in a narrow passage of water, and we doubt we will be able to cope. We forget that God has helped us through the "todays," and when "tomorrow" becomes "today," He will be there to help us through that one, too.

When I was younger, I often uttered a glib, home-made remedy to anyone concerned about handling a future problem. "When we get to the river, God builds the bridge," I would say, hopefully indicating that when we had the problem, God would take care of it, but His help wouldn't be there until we needed it.

When my ten-year-old-son heard me say that one day, he retaliated, "And don't make rivers that aren't there."

Isn't that what worry is all about? We conjure up problems (rivers) that don't yet exist. How will I pay the bills? How will I take care of the house? Or the children, or the car, or a dozen other responsibilities? We forget that God has helped us take care of "today's" problems, and we can trust Him to help us with the future ones. He doesn't give His strength in advance.

God's Word tells us we can look to the birds for reassurance. They don't "sow or reap or store away in barns, and yet your heavenly Father feeds them. Are you not much more valuable than they?" (Matthew 6:26 NIV).

Now God doesn't intend for us to treat life with abandonment. The birds also build their own nests, and they forage for their own food. But God takes care of their "needs," and we can trust Him to do the same for us.

Jesus also tells us that worrying doesn't do any good anyway. He asks the question, "Who of you by worrying can add a single hour to his life?" (Matthew 6:27 NIV). When I was a little child, I thought that worrying about something would help it not to happen, but of course I was so wrong.

Jesus does give us the solution, however, in His same discourse on the subject of worry: "Don't be anxious about tomorrow. God will take care of your tomorrow too. Live one day at a time (Matthew 6:34 TLB).

As the psalmist said, "Give your burdens to the Lord. He will carry them" (Psalm 55:22 TLB).

Dear Jesus, please help me not to ruin today by worrying about tomorrow.

Now is the time to trust.
WINFIELD FRANK RUELKE

23

THE FEAR FACTOR

Do not be afraid, for I am with you.
ISAIAH 43:5 NIV

About a month after my husband died, my son invited me to spend a few days with him at his home in another city. I appreciated the invitation, but he lived more than a hundred miles away, and the prospect of driving there alone made me panic.

It was only a little more than a two-hour drive on a well-marked four-lane freeway, but my husband had always done the long-distance driving. Now I would have to read the map, watch the road signs, and make sure the car had enough gas. I didn't mind driving around the environs where I lived, but tooling down a busy freeway with huge trucks was something else.

I determined, however, that I wouldn't let fear keep me home, and I made plans to undertake the venture. I prayed for courage, but the Lord didn't give me an answer till I was ready to go. Just before leaving, my eyes felt drawn to a magnet on my refrigerator door. A friend had given it to me for Christmas a couple of years before. It pictured two deer splashing through a country stream, and underneath a caption read: "Lord, help me remember that nothing is going to happen today that You and I can't handle."

God would be my copilot. I could trust Him to be with me on the freeway.

"Thank You, Jesus," I murmured. This was the reassurance I needed. I backed the car out of the garage and drove to my son's home with no problems.

This was the first of many accomplishments in which God would give me His help. Three years later, He even gave me the courage to sell my home and buy a house in the city where my son lived. We never know what we can do with God's help until we try it.

Every flight of stairs starts with the first step. What "flight of stairs" do you want to climb? Is having enough money a problem? Maybe you need help with yard work or home repairs. Is depression weighing you down? Whatever problem you want to overcome, or whatever task you want to accomplish, take that first step, and trust Jesus to help you up to the next one.

*Dear Jesus, please help me to
fear less and trust You more.*

*Courage is the capacity to go ahead
in spite of the fear.*
Scott Peck

24

A Traveling Companion

I will instruct you and teach you
in the way you should go.
PSALM 32:8 NIV

Driving a hundred miles to visit my son was not the thing I liked best to do, even though I knew God was with me as my copilot. I still wished I could have a more visible friend in the passenger seat beside me. I am certain the Lord knew my dilemma, and He helped me solve my problem.

When our local newspaper carried an article about the advantages of owning a dummy, I immediately felt this might be God's answer for me. I recognized that "male companionship" would be an asset, and perhaps a dummy of that gender would suffice. So I checked out the availability of the mannequin and purchased him for a hundred dollars. I named him Rick.

Rick's legs are detachable, which helps the portability factor. He looks muscular, and his broad shoulders stretch his shirt across his chest in a reassuring manner. His gray hair makes him look distinguished. I usually put sunglasses on him when we travel, and I let him hold the road map. He is quite tall—he sits higher than I do in the car—and his presence does give me confidence with my driving and helps me feel safer.

Sometimes I get rather strange looks from cars that

pass by. Some people wave, and others just laugh. Even though Rick never says a word, he is often the catalyst at rest stops that introduces me to strangers.

I have discovered that Rick is also quite a "companion" at home. When we're not driving together, Rick always sits in a reclining chair on my glassed-in patio. Night and day he sits there. Sometimes the meter man or the trash collector does a double take when seeing him, but that's okay. Any potential thief might do the same thing.

Really, Rick seems almost human. One day when my out-of-town son was visiting, he said, "You'd be surprised, wouldn't you, if one day Rick got up and moved." I told him I would indeed be surprised.

The next time I looked out to the patio, Rick was sitting in a different chair. It was my turn to do the double take—with my son laughing.

With a little imagination a homemade dummy could be easily created. A pillowcase stuffed with rags or old newspapers could serve as his body. Add a shirt and a coat, and this might be the start of an authentic traveling buddy. Perhaps an inflated balloon could be his head. With a hat pulled down low, passing cars might never know he was an airhead.

Perhaps there is a "dummy" in your future.

Lord, thank You for showing me
how to feel safer when I travel.

~

I always like to begin a journey on Sundays,
because I shall have the prayers of the Church
to preserve all that travel by land or by water.
JONATHAN SWIFT

25

ANGEL PROTECTION

For he will command his angles concerning you to guard you in all your ways.
<small>PSALM 91:11 NIV</small>

The loneliness that follows the loss of a loved one can sometimes prompt unrealistic fears. The empty house may even seem threatening. Isn't it great to know God's angels protect us! We can't see them with our physical eyes, but this doesn't mean they aren't there.

As I was pressing a dress in the basement, the phone near the ironing board rang. With the iron still in my hand, I picked up the receiver.

"A tall man is watching your house," an ominous-sounding male voice intoned on the other end of the line.

"What did you say?" I gasped, as my knees started to shake.

The husky voice slowly repeated his message.

Almost without thinking, I said, "That's okay. Angels are watching my house, too."

Angels are watching my house! A few days earlier I wouldn't have given that response, but just the day before, I had listened to a cassette tape of the ninety-first psalm. The eleventh verse assured me that God's angels were protecting me. Why should I fear a "tall man" (or anyone else) when angels were all around me?

For several weeks I had been receiving tapes on Revelation, which I had requested from a local church. That week the church secretary had "accidentally" sent me the Psalm tape instead of the one in Revelation.

As soon as I mentioned angel protection, the phone line went dead. I waited a few minutes, then went upstairs and looked out the window for reassurance. There was no "tall man" in sight.

I realized that the phone call was probably just a hoax—but I phoned the police anyway. They told me they had received several calls about such a voyeur, and there was no cause for concern. It was just a fabrication.

I was relieved by this pronouncement, but at the same time I praised God that He had prepared me ahead of time to put my trust in His protection.

Thank You for having Your angels protect us.

~

Everything we call a trial,
a sorrow, or a duty,
believe me, that an angel's hand is there.
FRA GIOVANNI

26

FROM PANIC TO PEACE

We are more than conquerors
through him who loved us.
<small>ROMANS 8:37 NIV</small>

After a friend at church lost her husband, she began to experience panic attacks. Leaving the comfort and safety of her home for any reason would usually precipitate one. She would start to sweat, the muscles in her throat would tighten, she would become short of breath, and her pounding heart felt as if it were trying to escape from her chest. She dreaded these episodes, and she began to be a prisoner in her own home.

Sometimes medical assistance is needed, for God provides doctors and medicines to help us, but we can also turn to our Lord as our Great Physician. Through Him we can become "more than conquerors."

Another friend was given this reassurance in the hospital when she was facing delicate thyroid surgery the next day. A young man from her church visited her that evening, and as he was preparing to leave, he said, "Remember Joshua 1:9." After he was gone, she reached for her Bible to find the verse.

"Be strong and courageous. Do not be terrified; do not be discouraged, for the LORD your God will be with you wherever you go" (Joshua 1:9 NIV). Moses gave this advice to Joshua before he entered the Promised Land.

Moses knew his younger replacement would be facing many battles and dangerous circumstances. The same God goes with us today to help us with the problems we can't handle alone.

I shared this with my friend who was having the panic attacks. I also gave her a little metal cross like the one I always carry to remind me that my Lord is with me wherever I go. A written Bible verse would serve the same purpose. This is why ancient Jews wrote Bible verses on bits of parchment and put them in little leather cases that they tied to their left arms or their foreheads. We humans often need tangible reminders to give us assurance.

Often we have to take the first step, and God meets us on the way. Joshua never would have known that God could help him conquer the Promised Land if he had never crossed the Jordan River. My friend never would have overcome her panic attacks if she had never left the house.

God also promises us His peace: Jesus said, "My peace I give you. I do not give to you as the world gives. Do not let your hearts be troubled and do not be afraid" (John 14:27 NIV).

*Thank You for the assurance You are always
with me, and please help me have Your peace.*

*To be glad of life,
because it gives you the chance
to love and to work and to play
and to look up at the stars,
to think every day of Christ. . . .
These are little guideposts
on the footpath to peace.*
HENRY VAN DYKE

27

GOD'S ARMOR

*Put on the full armor of God so that you can take
your stand against the devil's schemes.*
EPHESIANS 6:11 NIV

Jesus spent forty days and forty nights in the wilderness talking to His Father before He started His public ministry. At the end of that time, He was tired and very hungry. That was when Satan came to Him with enticing temptations (Matthew 4:1–11).

Likewise, if our grief prevents us from eating or sleeping adequately, we may be especially vulnerable to Satan's fiery darts. His weapons against us are doubt (*I'll never make it through life alone*), discouragement (*Nothing I do really counts for much*), lethargy (*Why try?*). Our struggle is not against flesh and blood but against spiritual forces (Ephesians 6:10–17), and we need to put on the full armor of God.

First, strap on the belt of truth for hand-to-hand combat with Satan. What truths do we know about God? For one thing, He is always with us. Hebrews 13:5 assures us He will never leave us. And He has unlimited power. "With God all things are possible" (Matthew 19:26 NIV). You can probably think of many more.

Next is the breastplate of righteousness. Our "breastplate" is our right relationship with God. According to

Psalm 66:18, if we harbor unconfessed sin, our Lord can't hear us. But 1 John 1:9 (NIV) assures us, "If we confess our sins, he is faithful and just and will forgive us our sins and purify us from all unrighteousness."

Our feet should be fitted with the readiness that comes from the gospel of peace. We need to have "shoes" that allow us to be ready for battle. Jesus told His disciples in John 16:33 (NIV), "In me you may have peace. In this world you will have trouble. But take heart! I have overcome the world." We, too, can claim His peace. It will help us to always be prepared to give an answer to everyone who asks a reason for the hope that we have (1 Peter 3:15).

Our shield of faith equips us to extinguish the "flaming arrows of the evil one" (Ephesians 6:16 NIV). First John 5:4 (NIV) says, "This is the victory that has overcome the world, even our faith."

The next two pieces of armor are especially essential to our spiritual battle with Satan: the helmet of salvation and the sword of the Spirit, which is the Word of God. If we have received Jesus as Savior, John 1:12 assures us we are children of God and our "helmet" is secure. And Hebrews 4:12 qualifies our sword: The word of God is living and active, sharper than any two-edged sword as it penetrates even to the dividing of soul and spirit.

Jesus defeated Satan with scripture—and we can do likewise.

*Lord Jesus, thank You for supplying me with
Your armor. Please help me be a conqueror.*

~

*The Bible is a book of faith,
and a book of doctrine, and a book of morals,
and a book of religion, of especial revelation
from God.*
DANIEL WEBSTER

28

A SPECIAL REFUGE

It is good to be near God. I have made
the Sovereign LORD my refuge.
PSALM 73:28 NIV

The Old Testament designated special places where people who had accidentally killed someone might escape the vengeance of outraged relatives or friends. These cities of refuge, as they were called, were available to everyone. Usually they were located on a hill where even a stranger to that area could find them. They were safe places, and unlike other cities, the gates were always open.

We, too, can have a "city of refuge" of a different kind, where we may escape the harassment of our grief and where we can find spiritual refreshment. Such a place is available to everyone. The "gates" are always open, and we will find that our Lord is constantly waiting there for us. As Psalm 34:18 (NIV) assures us, "The LORD is close to the brokenhearted and saves those who are crushed in spirit."

Our pastor has a special armchair in the basement of his house where he meets privately with Jesus. He doesn't go there to escape from grief, but that is his special "city of refuge" where he can elude the pressures of an arduous vocation. It is where he especially meets God in prayer, and where he often prepares his sermons.

I had a picnic table in one of the city's parks where I felt particularly close to God. Pine trees shielded the table from the street and made it a private place to worship. The table sat on a ledge overlooking a valley that rendered a panoramic view of our Lord's handiwork. I could see for miles, and as the vastness made me sense the omnipotence of our great God, I was so thankful that He loved me.

We can, of course, meet with our Lord in any locale and at any time, but it is helpful to have a designated place of rendezvous. A special closeness to Him seems realized when we join Him in a prearranged private place. It can be a specific location in your home where you have morning devotions, or it can be a pathway in the park where you stroll with Him at sunset. If you don't have such a place, you might enjoy finding one.

*Lord Jesus, help me find a place that is special
to just You and me.*

*Even in the low points,
my heart always runs to the Father
and finds peace only in Him.*
GWEN SHAMBLIN

29

THE THIRD-THUMB PROBLEM

*The LORD is my strength and my shield; my heart
trusts in him, and I am helped.*
PSALM 28:7 NIV

A few weeks after my friend Catherine lost her husband, she asked me one day, "How do you handle being a third thumb? Chet and I used to play bridge once a month with several couples, and I feel so out of place now when I am with them. Everyone tries to make me feel comfortable, but I feel I am just in the way."

I agreed it was a difficult adjustment. When we lose a loved one, life is never quite the same afterward. Someone who loses a spouse may feel awkward attending activities where there are only couples. That person has choices: go and remain uncomfortable, just stay home, or seek new friends and new activities. Libraries usually have a list of social functions that are eager for new members, or the Sunday newspaper will carry the agenda, the time, and the place of many activities. Anyone can call them up and ask if they want new attendees. This is how I discovered Stonecroft Ministries, which sponsors a monthly luncheon with a guest speaker.

For senior citizens, most communities have special activities for this age group. They may range from a monthly dinner meeting to a weeklong cruise. If further education is an interest, try taking a course at the local university or college. Anyone who is retirement age can usually monitor classes with no charge. And you meet all kinds of interesting people.

For anyone more adventuresome, fifty-five years old or older, Elderhostel may be an answer for wanted activity. This organization sponsors undertakings at universities, campsites, and other places throughout the United States and foreign countries. I know several people who have participated in their programs and have had a great time. You may want to look up Elderhostel on the Internet.

Even church may be a challenge to your comfort zone. Maybe joining a different Sunday school class is advisable. Instead of a couples class, change to a class that is all the same sex. At my church there is a singles class for those who are thirty plus, another for singles who are college age from eighteen to twenty-nine, and an all-women's class for those twenty years old and up. There is a class to fit every need.

At first you may feel out of place joining these different groups, but soon new friends will replace those left behind. You can trust the Lord for His help, and you will have a special Friend who will stay with you closer than a brother (Proverbs 18:24).

*Thank You that You are my special Friend
who will go everywhere with me.*

~

*Every true friend
is a glimpse of God.*
LUCY LARCOM

30

A Faith Fix

Let us run with perseverance the race marked out for us. Let us fix our eyes on Jesus, the author and perfecter of our faith.
HEBREWS 12:1–2 NIV

The Rubicon is a river in northern Italy. In violation of orders from leaders in Rome who feared his power, Julius Caesar crossed it with his army. He knew when he went over to the other side that he would never be able to return. As he did it, he is supposed to have said, "The die is cast" (referring to a roll of dice). A civil war followed, and Caesar emerged as ruler.

"Crossing the Rubicon" has become a general expression for taking a dangerous, decisive, and irreversible step. Have you made such a decision since the loss of your loved one?

For me, selling my home and buying a new house in a town more than a hundred miles away was my "crossing the Rubicon." There was no going back; another family was now living in the house where I had raised my family.

My new home was only a half mile from my son and his wife. This was the reason I had moved, and daily I counted the blessings of being near them. Also, organizing a new home challenged me: What drawers should I put things in, and where do I buy towels to match the new colors in the bathroom? The quest went on and on, and I determined to make it fun. I had lived in the same house for forty years, and I wanted the new change to be an adventure. As our Bible advises, I tried not to look back (Philippians 3:13), but rather to focus on the excitement of looking ahead.

At the top of my "to do" list was finding a church home. I intended to visit several churches before making a decision, but my second week sitting in church with my family cinched it. That was where I wanted to be.

Making new friends took awhile, but I discovered that God has His people everywhere. When I went to the post office to buy stamps, I commented to the man standing behind the counter that God had given us a beautiful day.

"Are you a Christian?" he asked.

"Yes, I am," I replied. For just a few minutes we talked about the Lord, and that was so refreshing to me. I had found a fellow believer at the post office. And this was just the first of many such rewarding experiences.

My husband had been gone three years before I decided to "cross the Rubicon." I had been advised that life-changing decisions should not be made immediately after the loss of a loved one, and I was glad I waited. Of course a "wait" is not always possible, but God's advice in Philippians 3:13 remains the same.

Dear Jesus, whatever You have waiting for
me in the future, help me to see it
as an adventure with You.

I avoid looking forward or backward,
and try to keep looking upward.
CHARLOTTE BRONTË

31

THE PLUG PEW

Let us not neglect our church meetings.
HEBREWS 10:25 TLB

The church I attend has more than a thousand members with two Sunday morning worship services in a large auditorium that is usually crowded. Sunday evening services and our pastor's midweek Bible studies have fewer participants and are held in a smaller chapel. I enjoy the vibrant Sunday-morning gathering, but the others provide more intimate fellowship.

In the chapel, the fifth pew from the front has an electrical outlet on the floor where an overhead projector or other equipment can be plugged in. Those of us who regularly sit there together have dubbed it "The Plug Pew," and it has become a source of merriment for us. We joke about having a pseudo "Plug Pew membership."

It is not a "closed" fraternity, but it is one that nobody wants to belong to. We are all widows, and we kid about the Plug Pew being the Widow's Bench. None of us take our marital status lightly, but it helps our outlook on life to add a little humor along the way.

This is the church I joined soon after moving to a new city to be near my son and his family. It is a gospel preaching, evangelistic church with sound doctrine, and I am glad to be part of it. Sunday school here is called

Bible fellowship, and as soon as I joined the church, I went to one of the adult classes. It was a couples' class of wives and husbands, but they made me feel welcome even though I was only half a couple. I did not feel out of place, and I appreciated the stimulus of an occasional male point of view.

For several weeks, however, I did not go to the Sunday evening service or the Wednesday night Bible study. When I finally decided to try them both, my effort was rewarded with a new joy. It is so true that by drawing near to God, He draws near to us (James 4:8).

The small-group setting afforded a fresh intimacy that cultivated new friends, such as those I became acquainted with in the Plug Pew. One of the best cures for loneliness is the acquisition of new friends, and the ideal place to find them is at church. No wonder God urges us to "not neglect our church meetings" (Hebrews 10:25 TLB).

*Lord, help me to be involved in the church
where You want me to be.*

~

*To be of no church is dangerous.
Religion, of which the rewards are distant,
and which is animated only by faith and hope,
will glide by degrees out of the mind unless it
be invigorated and reimpressed by external
ordinances, by stated calls to worship, and the
salutary influence of example.*
SAMUEL JOHNSON

32

PULLING TOGETHER

Praise be to the God and Father of our Lord Jesus Christ. . .who comforts us in all our troubles, so that we can comfort those in any trouble with the comfort we ourselves have received from God.
2 CORINTHIANS 1:3–4 NIV

Many people have found relief and comfort in joining a support group after losing a loved one. There is camaraderie and fellowship in associating with those who have had a similar traumatic experience. Several hospice associations sponsor such groups, and many hospitals do likewise. Many churches and some funeral homes also join the endeavor. Any of these sponsors can help you find such a group if you want one.

In addition to sharing their compassion, support groups can also share their knowledge on how they have coped with the changes their loss forced upon them. And as you share your compassion and knowledge with them, you find that you, too, are strengthened.

One of my friends took her stepchildren to a juvenile support group after the loss of their father, and she felt it was very helpful for them. One of the younger widows in my church found solace by inviting all the ladies who had lost loved ones to come to her home for a picnic in July. She owned a large home and several acres of land, and we enjoyed eating outside and sharing the warm evening together. This wasn't a regular support group, but sharing our experiences strengthened all of us, and it gave us cohesiveness at church that assured us we weren't fighting the battle alone.

The story is told of a mountain climber who became exhausted while battling an unexpected snowstorm on his attempt to reach the summit. He felt he just couldn't go on any further, and he resigned himself to the inevitable death he expected. He was ready to give up when he squinted through the blinding snow and discovered someone lying on the ground a short distance ahead of him. When he bent over the person who was half-buried in the snow, he found the man was still alive. He nudged him and the man responded with a moan.

The exhausted climber realized the man would freeze to death unless he was given help, and he started to massage the man's arms and legs to maintain their circulation. God gave him surprising strength, and as he worked to save the other man's life, he likewise saved his own. In the early dawn, when they were both rescued by the ski patrol, the exhausted climber realized he was alive because he had reached out to help another.

Support groups are similar in their mutual concern for one another.

If a support group would help me, or if I could help someone else, please lead me to the one You would have me to be in.

~

Trouble shared is trouble halved.
Dorothy Sayers

33

BLESSED ASSURANCE

Thou wilt keep him in perfect peace,
whose mind is stayed on thee.
Isaiah 26:3 KJV

Seventy-five Christians from various churches throughout the United States went to Jamaica for a weeklong mission endeavor. Some of them conducted vacation Bible schools at area churches. Others helped refurbish church buildings by constructing new pews and doing various painting jobs, both inside and out.

Four nights after they arrived, one of the men complained of feeling hot. His face became almost as red as a traffic light, and his entire body started to itch. Soon his lips began to tingle and become progressively numb. In less than twenty minutes, his tongue started to swell and his breathing became labored. The group leader's wife, who was a registered nurse, was summoned to help. As his condition worsened, his wife frantically tried to cool his body with ice. Other members of the group congregated nearby and began praying.

They soon realized they needed more help than any of them could give. Several of the men lifted him into a car, and they raced to the community hospital. A nurse there started an intravenous line, and the doctor ordered an injection of medicine that began to reverse his symptoms. In just a short time, his health returned to normal.

When his tongue had started swelling and breathing was becoming difficult, he felt he was going to die. As a born-again Christian, he knew if that happened he would be in the presence of the Lord. As he surrendered to God's will, a feeling of utter peace swept over him.

Almost at the same time, although they did not realize it until afterward, his wife, too, felt his life was slipping away. As she realized he might soon be with Jesus, a calming peace engulfed her also, and she was able to relinquish him to the Lord.

The Bible tells us to be absent from the body is to be present with the Lord (2 Corinthians 5:8). What a blessed assurance that is. We can know that our loved one is now experiencing perfect peace, and a peace beyond understanding (Philippians 4:7) can be ours also as we stay close to Jesus.

Lord, help me have Your peace.

~

If peace be in the heart,
the wildest winter storm
is full of solemn beauty.
C. F. RICHARDSON

34

Our Heavenly Home

You will fill me with joy in your presesnce, with
eternal pleasures at your right hand.
Psalm 16:11 niv

It is so hard to lose a loved one, but have you ever thought of what heaven must be like?

My friend who had become a quadriplegic following an accident so looked forward to heaven. There she would have a perfect body. She could walk again—even run—and there would be no more pain.

As soon as your loved one left you, he stepped into the Lord's presence. The transmission was immediate. Did not Jesus say to the thief on the cross in Luke 23:43 (NIV), "Today you will be with me in paradise"?

The apostle Paul fundamentally told the believers at Corinth the same thing in 2 Corinthians 5:8 (NIV), "We are confident, I say, and would prefer to be away from the body and at home with the Lord."

In a letter to the church at Philippi, Paul said he would really rather go on and be with the Lord, but he realized he was more help to the believers if he continued to live. He summed it up in Philippians 1:21 (NIV) by saying, "For to me, to live is Christ and to die is gain."

There are many things we do not know about heaven, but God has told us everything we need to know. He has told us how to get there: In John 14:6 (NIV) Jesus said, "I am the way and the truth and the life. No one comes to the Father except through me." And we know it is a prepared place, because in John 14:2 (NIV) He said, "In my Father's house are many rooms.... I am going there to prepare a place for you."

Can you imagine what it must be like to be in the actual presence of Jesus?

The last three years my mother lived, Alzheimer's clouded her mind till she had no knowledge of her surroundings. She didn't know anyone, including me. The disease had changed her from a loving, outgoing, compassionate person to a vacant shell. Her only reaction to any stimuli was opening her mouth when someone fed her. When the nursing home, where she had to live the last year of her life, called at five in the morning to tell me she had died, my immediate response was, "Praise the Lord." She now was with Jesus; she was whole again.

And someday we will join our loved ones in that special place.

Thank You, Jesus, for preparing heaven for us
and showing us how to get there.

~

I wanted no other heaven than Jesus,
who shall be my joy when I come there.
JULIAN OF NORWICH

35

The Need to Be Needed

*As we have opportunity, let us do good
to all people, especially to those who
belong to the family of believers.*
GALATIANS 6:10 NIV

The need to feel needed is often an important issue for anyone who has lost a loved one. Very often the last few weeks—sometimes months and even years—have been spent as caregiver. When that need no longer exists, life has an empty space like part of a book that has missed its printing. It is a vacuum, and unfortunately a vacuum seeks to be filled.

The last four months of my husband's illness demanded my total attention. I couldn't even leave the house to buy groceries unless someone else could be with him. Hospice provided a nurse's aide who came for three hours a week so I could take care of necessary errands. After the funeral, and after necessary chores of adjustment had been given consideration, a large part of my life became an empty vacuum. No longer did anyone need me.

A fundamental rule of physics states that nature abhors any vacuum, and something else immediately rushes in to fill any vacated space. For example, the car in our garage occupies a certain amount of space. When we move it to the driveway, air instantly rushes in to fill the unoccupied area.

The same principle applies in our lives. Unwanted feelings like self-pity, envy, depression, and a host of other defeating thoughts may rush in to usurp the empty space our loss has carved out. So what do we do about it? As soon as possible, a return to normal activities helps. I went back to attending church twice on Sundays and on Wednesday evenings. I joined an exercise class and started going to Toastmasters. The flurry of activity helped, but I still had the need to be needed.

Modern life offers many opportunities for service if we are willing. To name just a few, schools need adult mentors, the Big Brothers Big Sisters organization needs volunteers, and hospitals can always use some help. The most satisfying way "to be needed" for Christians, however, is serving our Lord in some capacity. Maybe it is helping to write the church's weekly newsletter or accompanying the pastor to call on new members. The particular niche I have found in my church is overseeing the tract ministry and being a Sunday morning "greeter" in the children's department. Hugs from the kids are a reward in themselves.

Always there are places where we are needed.

Dear Jesus, You know my abilities and my needs. Help me find just the right place where I can serve You the best.

~

*One can bear grief,
but it takes two to be glad.*
ELBERT HUBBARD

36

PUPPY LOVE

Love is patient, love is kind. It does not envy, it does not boast, it is not proud.
1 CORINTHIANS 13:4 NIV

Animals give us a special kind of love. They don't question our motives or our morals; they just love us for who we are. Dogs, especially, can offer rewarding companionship to anyone living alone.

After my husband died, several people suggested I acquire a dog. My two sons hinted they might present one to me as a birthday or Christmas gift. I adamantly told everyone I did not want a dog; I wanted to be free to travel. Of course that didn't do much for my loneliness, but I insisted I did not want a pet.

When my son's dog died, he and his wife were propelled into the search for another family pet. They like big dogs, and their quest centered on finding a giant schnauzer. My daughter-in-law consulted the Internet and found a breeder in a city about a hundred miles from us. Since going there involved about a three-hour drive, she invited me to go with her when she investigated the puppy purchase.

While the breeder talked with my daughter-in-law, a pregnant miniature white schnauzer sat beside me and gave me puppy kisses. My heart melted. I said wistfully, "I think I really would like to have a dog."

Then I quickly added, "But I want to be free to travel."

My astonished daughter-in-law said she would keep the dog for me when I wanted to travel. How could I resist? That was how I acquired Jewel, the miniature white schnauzer that has become so much a part of my life.

When I return home after being away for a few hours, Jewel is there to greet me. She is always excited to see me and generous with her puppy kisses. Of course she doesn't speak my language, but she definitely communicates her thoughts. On days when I don't feel well, her sympathetic understanding is evident by her gentle nudges with a soft paw and an occasional whimper. When I am working around the house, she follows me like a white shadow. She has certainly helped lessen my loneliness.

I enjoy taking care of her: feeding her, brushing her, going for short walks with her. It is so nice to be needed—again.

Have you considered sharing your life with a pet? In addition to his dog, my son has a cat, an Angora rabbit, a macaw, and two goldfish. Perhaps you would enjoy a pet in one of those varieties.

Lord, if a pet would help me be less lonely,
help me find just the right one.

~

All things bright and beautiful,
All creatures great and small,
All things wise and wonderful:
The Lord God made them all.
CECIL F. ALEXANDER

37

THE "WAIT" COMPONENT

They that wait upon the LORD shall renew their strength. They shall mount up with wings like eagles; they shall run and not be weary; they shall walk and not faint.

ISAIAH 40:31 TLB

After losing a loved one, we may wonder if the depression and sorrow we are feeling will ever be lifted. Our days may seem as dark and foreboding as a continuing storm, one day after another. We may think, *Is there any hope I will ever be happy again?*

The onslaught of grief is normal, but with God's help, bearing it does become easier as time progresses—and yes, we will find happiness again. The Bible tells us there is "a right time for everything. . . . A time to cry; a time to laugh; a time to grieve; a time to dance" (Ecclesiastes 3:1, 4 TLB). This "timing" may be different for each person.

My grandmother frequently produced homemade bread for her family. She would stir together all the ingredients, then dump them onto a floured board and knead them for several minutes. When the dough became a soft, rounded mass, she would flip it back into the bowl, cover it with a cloth, and let it rise till it doubled in size. The humidity and temperature in the kitchen would influence how rapidly it would rise, and Granny would frequently check its progress.

Then she would deflate the bloated mound and

shape the dough into rolls or loaves and set them aside to puff up till they, too, were doubled in size. Afterward, baking them in a hot oven produced a delightful, tantalizing aroma throughout the entire house. Later her family always enjoyed her production.

Just as Granny needed to wait for her dough to rise before she could shape it into bread for her family, we, too, need to wait while God heals our hurt. Circumstances may vary this timing, but we have the assurance that our Lord checks on our progress just as Granny checked on her bread.

Waiting is never easy, but we have God's promise that He will "renew our strength." He will enable us to live above our circumstances just as eagles fly above turbulent weather conditions. He will help us to run and not be weary, to walk and not faint.

A friend recently told me that he felt a better translation for Philippians 4:13 is: "I can *endure* everything through him who gives me strength" rather that "I can *do* everything." Yes, God can help us to *endure* the wait.

*Waiting is so difficult. Please give me patience
as You help me heal the hurt.*

~

*He who knows patience
knows peace.*
CHINESE PROVERB

38

MOMENTS OF MEMORY

I thank my God every time I remember you.
PHILIPPIANS 1:3 NIV

Our tears are often near the surface after we lose a loved one. A familiar song that evokes a memory may make our eyes moist. An object around the house that suddenly reminds us of a shared experience may prompt us to cry. This is part of the "grief process," but what we do with it makes a big difference.

The above scripture is taken out of context, but the words can be an avenue of advice for us. Each time a memory pricks our minds, we can thank God for our past happiness—or we can feel sorry for ourselves and be resentful of our loss. If we concentrate on gratitude for our past pleasures, those memories can be comforting blessings.

Lemon meringue pie is something that has called forth memories for me. My husband's favorite dessert was that kind of pie. I liked it, too, but I wasn't as passionate about it as he was. As we grew older, we both tried to be careful of calories, so we often shared a piece of his favorite pie when we had dinner together in a restaurant. Now if I see lemon meringue pie on a menu, I usually order it and savor each bite as I remember the good times I have had with my husband. I am thankful that God gave me those years with him; some people never have such blessings.

A familiar song is often the most poignant of memory pricks. For me, it has been "Victory in Jesus." It was my husband's favorite song. It outlines the joys that will be found in heaven, and as the effects of his cancer became more oppressive, he realized he would soon be experiencing these joys. If the congregation sang that hymn in church, he would usually reach for my hand and hold it as a special assurance to me that he knew where he was going. It would be a victory, not a defeat, because he knew Jesus as his personal Savior.

Several times he told me he wanted "Victory in Jesus" sung at his funeral. He wanted it to be a witness to those who were not Christians. So I had the words of the song printed on the back page of the order of the service, and at the close of his funeral, we all stood to sing the hymn together.

Sometimes finding joy in memories is a challenge, but it is worth the effort.

*Lord, help me to find happiness in
the memories You give me.*

*God gave us memories that we
might have roses in December.*
JAMES M. BARRIE

39

A Tested Strength

But the Lord stood at my side and gave me strength.
2 Timothy 4:17 NIV

My friend Connie and I made plans to go to the hospital to visit a fellow church member who had recently suffered a heart attack and stroke. The next day she called me and said her mother would like to go with us.

"That might be hard for her to do," I replied. I knew her mother's husband had died in the same hospital about three months before. He had been in ICU thirty-four days following open-heart surgery, and she had practically lived at the hospital the whole time.

"I told her that," Connie said, "but she wants to do it anyway."

On our appointed day, Connie and her mother first stopped by my house, and then we drove to the hospital. On the way we engaged in casual chitchat and carefully avoided any sensitive subject. The visit with our friend went well. He was able to walk down to the lounge with us, and we talked with him for about a half hour.

On the way back home, I asked Connie's mother if being at the hospital again was difficult for her.

"I was a little spongy," she said. "But I am glad I

went. I couldn't have done it a month ago."

Returning to a hurtful venue after the loss of a loved one is often the best thing to do. The timing for undertaking it, however, differs with each person—just as an open sore requires a definite schedule when a therapeutic salve should be applied. But to constantly avoid going there may create a phobia that grows to unrealistic proportions. Go, and God will help you have the strength to do it. Sometimes the longer the delay, the more "strength" that is needed, and the fear can become a phobia.

Several places besides hospitals might evoke hurtful memories for you. The death of a friend may obligate you to go to calling hours at a funeral home. It will be especially difficult if it is the same funeral home where you stood beside the casket of your loved one. Or maybe the visit to a theater where you and your loved one enjoyed the performances will be hard for you. The first time you return to such a place will be the most difficult. You will probably feel as "spongy" as my friend's mother did, but God will help you do it, and afterward you will sense a victory.

Life goes on, and we need to be a part of it.

Dear Lord, thank You that You will
give me strength when I need it.

Each of us may be sure that
if God sends us on stony paths
He will provide us with strong shoes,
and He will not send us out on any journey
for which he does not equip us well.
ALEXANDER MACLAREN

40

CLAIMING CHRISTMAS CHEER

For to us a child is born, to us a son is given.
ISAIAH 9:6 NIV

Christmas is probably the most difficult holiday to handle after losing a loved one. Memories of past Yuletides crowd our minds, and tears are near the surface, especially if our loss is a recent one.

So what do we do about it? If decorating your home seems like an impossible task, maybe older children could do it for you in an innovative way. Or maybe the purchase of new decorations that wouldn't hold memories would be helpful. Possibly a table tree instead of the usual one that reached the ceiling would be a good choice. Leaving your house completely devoid of all Christmas remembrances, however, will only intensify the melancholy that already threatens you.

I was fortunate to be able to spend the first Christmas after my husband's death with my out-of-town son and his family. Three active grandchildren certainly helped to distract me from a memory overload. Maybe you can do the same thing.

If such an escape isn't possible, maybe you could spend the day at a rescue mission helping others to enjoy a special dinner and a moderately festive holiday. My husband and I did this one year after our grown children had left home and spending the day in our "empty nest" didn't seem attractive.

Maybe an invitation for friends or relatives to share the day with you might be a pleasant alternative to solitude with just your memories. If there is a university in the city where you live, there are probably out-of-state students who would welcome being with you. Foreign students might be even more grateful.

If you enjoy baking, producing a small gift of Christmas cookies for your neighbors might bring holiday happiness to you as well as to them. Your church can probably use extra help during this season, and possibly you could work with the children to present a skit or help out with their choirs. One year the Bible fellowship from my church went to a nursing home to sing carols for the patients and their visitors. Maybe you could initiate a similar endeavor at your church.

There are many ways to bring Christmas cheer to others, and in a wonderful way that same cheer always reverberates back to those who are giving it. "Give, and it will be given to you," God's Word tells us (Luke 6:38 NIV). This is especially true at Christmastime, when we remember the priceless gift God gave us when He sent His Son to earth to be our Savior.

*Please help me to have Your joy,
and show me how to share it with others.*

*It is Christmas in the heart
that puts Christmas in the air.*
W. T. ELLIS

41

ROSES AND THORNS

No matter what happens, always be thankful.
1 THESSALONIANS 5:18 TLB

When my husband was ill with cancer, a plaque in his oncologist's office pictured a long-stemmed red rose with prickly-looking thorns. A caption read, "We can complain because roses have thorns, or be thankful that thorns have roses."

I have often thought of that plaque since my husband died. It reminds me that I have a choice to make. I can look at the "thorns" and complain because I am lonely, or I can look at the "roses" and be thankful I have family and friends who love me. I can complain about my empty house or be thankful I have a house. I can complain to God because He allowed my husband to die, or I can thank Him for His assurance of eternal life.

A young pastor I know had been short of breath for several days. He thought his chronic asthma was causing it. His pulmonologist, however, felt it was a heart problem, not asthma, and ordered a stress test. The next day during the stress test, the pastor had a heart attack and collapsed. CPR was performed, and a short time later he had open-heart surgery for five bypasses. In the recovery room afterward his condition deteriorated, and doctors brought him back to the operating room to install a life-support device that pumped his heart for him. He was considered for a heart transplant. Doctors expressed cautious optimism that he wouldn't need it, but he was transferred from the local hospital to a special heart clinic in another city.

All this happened in early June. In August he was still hospitalized. His condition had improved to where he could walk a little, but breathing was sometimes difficult, and a slight stroke had left him unable to swallow. His wife stayed in a facility a block away from the hospital, and she was with him almost every day. Each night she reported his condition on the hospital Web site that kept family and friends advised of their patients' conditions.

One of her entries near the end of August read as follows: "God is here with us in this place. We see Him in the kind hearts and warm smiles of so many. Tonight He smiled and giggled with me through the face of the most beautiful four-month-old baby. The baby is here with his mother on the same floor where I am staying, and he is a precious gift to each one of us. Thank You, Lord."

Always there is a rose among the thorns.

Lord, help me see the "roses" not the "thorns."

*Afflictions are but the
shadow of God's wings.*
GEORGE MACDONALD

42

A Thankful Heart

It is a good thing to give thanks unto the LORD,
and to sing praises unto thy name, O most High.

PSALM 92:1 KJV

With this age of electronics, I have friends who seem to feel compelled to send e-mails to me. They send me stories gleaned from the Internet, news articles, and jokes. Occasionally they send something that really blesses my day. This is the way it was when I received the story about a group of students who were asked to list what they thought were the present "Seven Wonders of the World."

There were some disagreements, but their list included such human achievements as the Empire State Building and natural wonders like the Grand Canyon. One student, however, took an exceptionally long time in completing her inventory. When the teacher inquired if she was having a problem, she replied she couldn't make up her mind because there were so many.

The teacher said, "Tell us what you have, and maybe we can help."

Hesitantly the girl read her list. The first "wonder" she noted was "to see." The e-mail pictured a smiling young girl examining a fresh tulip on a clear, sunny day.

Her next blessing was "to hear." The accompanying

picture was a cheerful-looking young man strumming a banjo and singing.

"To touch" was the next assessment. The picture was a small baby crawling on a thick carpet and reaching out to lightly touch the furry paw of a collie puppy.

"To taste" was next. A little girl lying on her stomach in a grassy meadow and a schnauzer puppy were sharing the ice cream cone she was holding.

"To feel." A young mother clasped the tiny hands of her infant child.

"To laugh." A toddler, hardly old enough to sit upright, was giggling as he fingered a puppet doll.

"To love" was the last notation. The picture was a young man and woman holding hands as they frolicked through pink flowers on a hillside meadow. Her white gown and bouquet of orchids intimated they were recently married.

The schoolroom was quiet as the student finished her survey. It had made them realize the inherent wonder of so many blessings they had taken for granted.

Sometimes our burden of sorrow likewise squelches our gratitude to God for His daily blessings. There is no greater remedy for grief than a thankful heart, and praising God dissolves our gloom as the rising sun dissipates the morning dew.

Lord Jesus, please forgive my lack of gratitude.
I do praise You, and I thank You for Your love
and Your many blessings.

~

Gratitude is one of those things
that cannot be bought.
LORD HALIFAX

43

A BLESSINGS BOX

Praise the LORD, O my soul,
and forget not all his benefits.
PSALM 103:2 NIV

Often we fail to notice the "benefits" our Lord gives us, especially the little ones we have become accustomed to: fresh drinking water, clean clothes to wear, family and friends who love us, a church where we can worship. The list goes on and on, and our burdens don't seem quite so heavy if we remember the blessings God gives us.

When my husband was ill in the latter days before our Lord took him home, a friend gave me a blessings box. It was a covered, oblong-shaped box about five inches long that my friend decorated with lace and ribbons. Attached to it was the following poem:

When you're high atop the mountain
and the world seems bright and clear,
Why not write the Lord a "Thank You" note
and place the pages here.

And when the trials of life begin—
Although you didn't ask it,
Why not reach inside and count again
The blessings in this basket [box].

I don't know who wrote the poem, but it is a formula that helps to lift the clouds in a not-so-sunny day. Recognizing God's "little blessings" and writing a short note to thank Him for them helps to give awareness of their presence. Then on a "cloudy day," taking that note from the box and rereading it helps to chase away the gloom.

A blessings box doesn't need to be fancy. An empty shoebox with a notepad and pencil beside it does just fine. It's the principle, not the props, that makes the difference.

Perhaps the "blessing" is just a phone call from a friend, but on a day when you have no calls and loneliness seems to envelop you, it helps to read the note that assures you of a friend's love. Maybe one of the notes is about a special card that came one day in the mail, and rereading it helps to brighten your day when the mailbox is empty.

Maybe the Lord's presence seemed especially real to you during a church service or while you were praying, and rereading a "blessing note" about this helps you on those days when God may seem far away. A hot cup of coffee on a cold day may become a blessing note to remind you that God is taking care of your needs.

Lord, help me recognize the blessings You give me, and help me have a thankful heart.

~

I owe thee much. . . .
Far, far beyond
what I can ever pay.
ROBERT BLAIR

44

THE COMFORT OF CONTENTMENT

*I have learned to be content
whatever the circumstances.*

PHILIPPIANS 4:11 NIV

What does it mean to be content? The dictionary interprets it as being happy with what one has or is; satisfied. God's Word interprets it as accepting our status in life because we have the assurance that our Lord is with us.

You may be familiar with the Serenity Prayer:

God grant me the Serenity
to accept the things
I cannot change...
Courage to
change the things I can...
and Wisdom to
know the difference.

This prayer has given comfort and encouragement to people for many years. Its origin is unknown, but one of the theories that has stockpiled about it credits an Alcoholics Anonymous member with giving it to Bill Wilson, cofounder of that organization, in 1939. When he and his staff read the prayer, they felt it particularly suited the needs of AA. It became an integral part of the movement, and each meeting began by reciting it.

After the loss of a loved one we, too, need to accept the things we cannot change. There is no way we can bring our loved one back to us. But with God's help we can change the future, and He will give us the wisdom to know what we should do. Likewise, He will grant us His contentment.

In 1956 five young missionaries—Pete Fleming, Roger Youderian, Ed McCully, Nate Saint, and Jim Elliot—went into the Amazon jungle in Ecuador to tell the natives there about the love of Jesus. They particularly wanted to reach the savage Auca tribe that no one had ever been able to go into. For months they prepared the way by airlifting small gifts to them, and finally on January 3 they established a beachhead in Auca territory. At first the natives' reception seemed cautiously friendly, but five days later all five missionaries were speared to death.

The widows of the five young men could not change the tragedy, but they could change their situation. One, Elisabeth Elliot, remained in the jungle and continued to work for the redemption of the barbaric tribes. She was joined by Nate Saint's sister, Rachel. Ultimately they were able to live among the Aucas for almost a year, and several tribesmen came to know Jesus as their Savior. Another widow, Marj Saint, remained as a missionary in Quito.

In the midst of all the danger and discomfort, they declared they were content. Like the apostle Paul, they had an inward peace doing what the Lord wanted them to do. And that same contented peace can be ours, too, as we stay close to Jesus.

Lord Jesus, show me the path You would have me take, and help me be content.

~

*Resolve to see the world
on the sunny side,
and you have almost won the
battle of life at the outset.*
SIR ROGER L'ESTRANGE

45

FINDING JOY

Weeping may endure for a night,
but joy cometh in the morning.
PSALM 30:5 KJV

The depression that often follows the loss of a loved one may seem like one continuous dark night. You may feel you will never smile, or laugh, again, but just as the dawn dissipates the black shroud of night, God's love can dispel the sorrow that engulfs your life.

Vickie Baker discovered the secret to finding joy. She didn't lose a loved one; she lost her life. Or at least she felt she had. She was a trapeze performer in a circus, and she loved doing it. She had been hooked on "flying through the air with the greatest of ease" since a friend had urged her to try the trapeze at a YMCA. But five years later, while practicing a two-and-a-half-turn somersault for her circus act, a split-second mistake changed her life forever. She didn't tuck her head under as she was supposed to do, and she plunged headfirst into a net and dislocated her spinal cord. Instantly she became a quadriplegic.

This was more than she could handle; it was her "black night." During the next three years she made three unsuccessful attempts at suicide. When she landed in the psych ward of a local hospital, she finally reached out to God. Finding Jesus changed her life again, but this time for the better.

I met Vickie at a writers' conference in Colorado, and she radiated the joy of the Lord. We became e-mail friends afterward, and always her correspondence reflected her joy. Despite being bound to a wheelchair and needing the continuing care of an attendant, her joy spilled over and touched the lives of countless others.

God gave Vickie a ministry of encouragement that reached around the world. Via the computer she wrote hundreds of letters to share her joy with prison inmates and with those who suffered disabilities. She published a charming book of poems and vignettes titled *On Wings of Joy*, and she told her life story in *Surprised by Hope*.

God may not give you a ministry of letter writing, but He gives each of us a "ministry." It may not be more than sharing a cup of coffee with a neighbor, but doing it with the love of Jesus is a ministry. Even a mere smile can be one. A smile is the most contagious thing in the world. Always it will be returned to the sender, and it blesses the one who gives it and the one who receives it.

As Nehemiah said, "The joy of the LORD is your strength" (Nehemiah 8:10 NIV).

Thank You for Your provision that
I will be able to laugh again.

Laughter is the closest thing
to the grace of God.
KARL BARTH

46

CHURCH SLIPPERS

A cheerful heart is good medicine.
PROVERBS 17:22 NIV

Sunday morning I usually flop around in my slippers until time to leave for church. Slippers are more comfortable than dress shoes, and usually the maneuver works very well. One Sunday morning, however, a last-minute phone call created a distraction. When I hung up the receiver, I glanced at the kitchen clock and discovered I was ten minutes late in leaving.

Hurriedly I picked up my Bible and dashed out the door to the car. When I arrived at the church, I discovered I was still wearing my well-worn slippers. My first reaction was horror. My second one was a strong desire to return home and change footwear.

The latter was impossible. I lived a twenty-minute drive from the church, and I was scheduled to be a greeter that day at the door. The only alternative to wearing slippers would be going barefoot, and that didn't seem an advisable choice.

Hoping no one would notice my feet, I obligingly took my post at the door. "Good morning," I said with extra emphasis to the first person who came toward me.

That "person" was an observant teenager who immediately noticed my breach in fashion.

"Did you break your toe?" he asked.

"No, no," I replied, "I'm just starting a new fashion in footwear."

The teenager laughed. I laughed, too. Maybe the situation wasn't as appalling as I thought.

To the next person who noticed my social blunder, I replied with the same explanation. I even kicked up one foot to emphasize my proclamation. And like the teenager, that person laughed, too.

By the time church was ready to begin, half the congregation had observed my slippers and laughed about it. I laughed, too. And it taught me a lesson: look for the humor in life and learn to laugh. As the Bible says, "A cheerful heart is good medicine." God gave us a sense of humor for a reason.

No matter how dim your situation seems to be, try to search out something that is "cheerful." Can you remember something your grandchildren said that was funny? Have you watched a squirrel trying to outsmart his feathered competitors at the bird feeder? Is there a television program that made you laugh in the past and might provide lighthearted humor for you now?

It's okay to laugh again. Your loved one would want you to.

It would be so nice to laugh again.
Lord, help me be able to do it.

~

Laughter is the sun
that drives winter
from the human face.
Victor Hugo

47

THE LIGHT EFFECT

"I am the light of the world."
John 8:12 NIV

Soon after high school graduation, Dale Chihuly went to the University of Washington in Seattle to study interior design and architecture. While there, he learned how to melt and fuse glass. The versatility of glass fascinated him, and in a later college course he experimented with incorporating glass shards into woven tapestries. After earning his degree in interior design, he established his own basement studio where he found he could blow a glass bubble by melting stained glass and using a metal pipe.

Chihuly continued to experiment with glassblowing. He studied at several universities and took advantage of learning from accomplished mentors. Today he is a glass artisan of world renown. When I heard on TV that our local conservatory was planning an exhibit of his work, I wanted to see it.

Dates for the display coincided with a visit from two of my out-of-town friends. When I told them about this unique opportunity of seeing Chihuly's work, they, too, wanted to go to the conservatory.

They weren't disappointed. Vibrant glass sculptures of differing hues and many colors nestled among the lush plant life of the conservatory. Large, multicolored glass blossoms looked like enormous tropical flowers. Glass spears, rods, tubes, and twirls peered from behind verdant foliage as if they were giant jungle blossoms. We spent the entire afternoon drinking in the beauty of one man's artistry and God's creative handiwork.

Three days after my friends left to go home, my son and daughter-in-law invited me to go to the conservatory with them. They realized I had been there a short time before, but they thought perhaps I would like to see the exhibit at night. I told them I would love to go back, day or night.

I had thought Chihuly's display was beautiful in the daytime, but that was nothing compared to its exquisite radiance as it basked in the glow of countless lights. It reminded me of the difference that comes into our lives when we choose to let Christ bathe us in His light. It is this Light that can touch our sorrow and change it into a joy that only He can give.

*Dear Jesus, thank You that You
came to give light to our world,
which is sometimes so very dark.*

~

*Even in the winter,
even in the midst of the storm,
the sun is still there.*
GLORIA GAITHER

48

LIGHTED SHADOWS

*"Whoever follows me will never walk in darkness,
but will have the light of life."*
JOHN 8:12 NIV

Have you ever noticed that there are no shadows on a cloudy day? That is because the sun is hiding above the clouds. During days when depression seems to be bearing down on you like ominous storm clouds, the reason may be that they have hidden the Son.

When a plane gains altitude and penetrates beyond the clouds, the passengers bask in the rewarding presence of brilliant sunshine. We can do the same thing with our "cloudy" days. We can rise above the depression that plagues us and enjoy our fellowship with the Son.

On bright, sunny days, the dark shadows that dance around us also have a message. When the sun is in the east, the west side of my home is shaded. In the early morning when the sun hangs low in the eastern sky, the shadow from the house extends far across the lawn. As the sun climbs higher, the shadow begins to dwindle.

At high noon there are no shadows. They disappear in the noonday brightness.

In the afternoon the shadows once again appear. A lengthening shadow extends from the other side of the house and settles across that lawn. As the sun marches slowly across the western sky and descends into the horizon, the shadows migrate into darkness.

The length of the shadows depends on the positioning of the sun and the strength of its rays. How similar this is to the problems that seem to cast long shadows over the happiness we wish we could find. As we let the Son come into our lives, His light dispels our darkness just as the approach of the noonday sun shrivels the shadows beneath it.

Our day always goes better when we begin it with Jesus. A quiet time with Him begins to light our soul the way the dawn starts to chase away the dark night. And throughout the day, the light of the Son can banish the depression and the dark thoughts that shadow our minds.

I always keep a little metal cross in the pocket of my slacks to remind me that Jesus is with me. When a problem starts to be an encroaching "shadow," I slip my hand into my pocket, and the cold metal of the tiny cross reminds me that the Son is with me.

The Bible tells us that when we draw near to Him, He draws near to us (James 4:8).

Dear Jesus, I want Your light in my life.
Help me to stay close to You.

Hope is like the sun, which,
as we journey toward it,
casts the shadow of our burden behind us.
SAMUEL SMILES

49

OUR REFLECTED LIGHT

"Let your light shine before men, that they may see your good deeds and praise your Father in heaven."
MATTHEW 5:16 NIV

The moon has no light of its own, but it shines because sunlight reflects from its surface.

Our lives are much like the moon. We have no "light" in ourselves, but God allows us to reflect the light of Jesus to others.

One day when Jesus was speaking to crowds of people, He told them He was the "light of the world." Then He added, "Whoever follows me will never walk in darkness, but will have the light of life" (John 8:12 NIV).

What a precious gift Jesus gives us. And He grants us the privilege of sharing that "light" with others. As our "good works" bless other people, they are drawn to our Savior and praise our Father in heaven.

Periodically an eclipse of the moon occurs, and its light can no longer be seen. This happens as the earth's shadow obstructs the moon's reflection of the sun. Likewise, it is a challenge to us not to let our grief be such a dense "shadow" that it obstructs God's "light" to those around us.

For more than forty years, Margaret and Willard Grant were youth evangelists who traveled throughout the United States to tell young children about Jesus.

Their lively programs always included songs, stories, marionettes, and hand-painted pictures. They helped hundreds of children to ask Jesus to "come into their hearts."

After retirement, they continued to work vigorously for their Lord—even through the three years when Willard was ill and surgeries were limiting. Always the question foremost in their minds was, "What does the Lord want me to do?"

After God called Willard to his eternal home, Margaret asked that same question of herself. She has continued to work for her Lord in much the same way as she had done when Willard was with her. As the Holy Spirit inspires her, she plans and produces programs, writes scripts, and tells stories each week to the Awana children at her church. She shares devotions and sermons with those who ask her to do it, and she has made decorations for chapels and banquets.

She desperately misses Willard, but she has not let the "shadow" of her grief keep her from serving her Lord. And God can help you to do likewise. You may not be called upon to write scripts and plan programs, but as you ponder His direction for your life, He will lead you in the way you should go (Proverbs 3:6).

Dear Jesus, please help me share
Your light with others.

Nor sink those stars in empty night:
They hide themselves in heaven's own light.
JAMES MONTGOMERY

50

THROUGH THE MAZE

I will counsel you and watch over you.
PSALM 32:8 NIV

Every autumn, in the area where I live, several farmers convert their cornfields into mazes after the corn has been harvested. People come from many miles to accept the challenge of finding a route through the tall stalks. Sitting in an observation tower at the edge of the maze, the farmer watches their progress. If anyone becomes too frustrated with the winding trails, he will supply a solution to the dilemma.

The participants wend their way through the paths. If they try a route that dead-ends, they return to the fork in the road and try another way. This is like the pathways many of us take through the maze of grief after the loss of our loved ones. We try one thing after another with the hope we will again find happiness, and sometimes it seems that all roads are blocked. But like the pilgrims through the maze, when one pathway dead-ends, we need to return to the "fork in the road" and try another way.

Several people have found that a new venture is the "road" that leads them to happiness. After her mother died, one woman in a town near me used her story-telling ability to help others deal with grief at a hospice that rendered aid to her when she needed it. Twice a month during the school year she spends an hour or more on Thursday nights with families, teenagers, or groups of children. She often uses puppets to illustrate her stories about family, love, and loss. Nearly two thousand families have benefited from the program, and she loves what she is doing.

Telling stories to children might be a dead-end road for many of us. But we shouldn't lose heart. God may have a different pathway through the maze for us.

When a young woman from my church was on a Western vacation with her husband, he had a sudden heart attack and died. Of course, at first she felt devastated, but she allowed God to pick up the pieces of her life, and she enrolled in college to study for a career she had aborted when she was married. Later, she went to a seminary and studied to be an assistant pastor in a women's ministry.

This road also might not be the one that would bring you out of the maze of grief, but God can help you find another one. Just as the farmer in the observation tower sits high up to help those who become frustrated in his cornfield maze, God is watching over you and will help you through your "maze." And you can be certain that He knows the right pathway.

Thank You for watching over me.

*Still round the corner
there may wait,
a new road,
or a secret gate.*
J. R. R. TOLKIEN

51

THE GOURD'S HIDDEN QUALITY

*The God of all grace. . .will himself restore you and
make you strong, firm and steadfast.*
1 PETER 5:10 NIV

Gourds come in various sizes and shapes, but they all have a few things in common. When they are first taken from the ground, they are scarred and dirty. They may have a few ugly bumps or be misshapen in some other way. Inside they contain pulp and seeds that need to be cleaned out if the inside of the gourd is to be finished.

The daughter of one of the women in my church transforms these ugly-looking gourds into objects of beauty. First, she washes away the dirt and grime from their exteriors. Using sandpaper, she converts their bumps into smooth surfaces. She may use a saw, a drill or a knife to alter their shapes. Various colors of paint enhance her arsenal for metamorphosis. Patiently she spends time and energy to convert them into crafts that people enjoy.

She has made several birdhouses by removing the pulp and seeds from inside the gourds and creating circular entranceways. Smaller gourds have become painted dishes, sometimes decorated with contrasting borders. A plump round gourd has become a jolly Santa to help spread Christmas cheer. A long, rather awkward-looking gourd has become a cornucopia that would make a charming decoration for any Thanksgiving banquet. Even small, broken pieces—chiseled leftovers from the other crafts—have become useful objects of beauty. She has fashioned these into necklaces and brooches.

After we lose a loved one, we may feel like an ugly, bumpy, misshapen gourd that is of no use to anyone. But in the hands of our Creator, we can be made beautiful and productive. Sometimes the methods He uses, however, are not what we would like to see happening. His brand of "sandpaper" to smooth out some of our "bumps" may be painful.

God is in the business of refining us. He is the Master Carpenter. Just as the discarded pieces of the gourds can be fashioned into lovely necklaces and brooches, God can take the "pieces" of our shattered lives and mold them into something beautiful. But we have to submit to the chiseling methods He may use, always trusting He will restore our lives and make us strong, firm, and steadfast (1 Peter 5:10).

God has a beautiful blueprint for the rest of your life.

Lord, please take the pieces of my life and mold them into what You want me to be.

From all who dwell below the skies
Let the Creator's praise arise.
Isaac Watts

52

THE GIVING TREE

"Give, and it will be given to you. A good measure, pressed down, shaken together and running over, will be poured into your lap."
LUKE 6:38 NIV

My son and daughter-in-law attend a church that sponsors a fun family night three times during the summer. This includes a light, snack-type dinner and homespun entertainment. The entertainment usually consists of several skits in which the actors are church members.

In the last presentation of the season, my daughter-in-law helped present the skits. In one of them she raised her arms above her head and clasped her hands to become a "Giving Tree."

A young boy skipped onto the stage from behind a screen, and a narrator told how much the child enjoyed climbing up the tree's trunk, swinging from its branches, and eating its apples. The boy loved the tree, and the tree was happy.

Time went by, the boy grew older, and the tree was often alone. When he came back as a teenager, the tree invited him to swing from its branches, but the youth retorted he was too old to climb trees and play. He confided he wanted to earn money to buy some things, and the tree suggested that he could sell its apples. As he gathered the apples and carried them away, the tree once again was happy.

The boy was a young husband the next time he visited the tree. When he told it he needed to build a house for his wife and children, the tree volunteered the wood in its branches. My daughter-in-law lowered her arms to her side to demonstrate how her branches were used to fashion his house, and the narrator said, "Once again the lonely tree was happy."

The boy was quite elderly the next time he returned to the tree. This time he wistfully said he wanted to make a boat so he could sail away and be happy. "Cut down my trunk and make your boat," the tree said. My daughter-in-law slumped to the floor, indicating he did just that, and the narrator said, "Once again the lonely tree was happy."

With only a stump remaining, the tree still found happiness in being useful. When the boy came back as an old, old man, he sat on the stump and enjoyed a much-needed rest.

To feel needed is a great blessing, and opportunities to serve abound: assisting in the church office, helping to deliver Meals on Wheels, volunteering to babysit a grandchild. As we give away ourselves in helping others, God fills the vacuum with His happiness.

Lord, show me how to give away myself,
and help me to be filled with Your joy.

To have joy one must share it—
happiness was born a twin.
LORD BYRON

53

THE CLIPPER'S SOLACE

*"Blessed are those who mourn,
for they will be comforted."*
<small>MATTHEW 5:4 NIV</small>

Our Lord sometimes finds unexpected ways to comfort us. As the first anniversary of my husband's death drew close, tears were always near the surface. Every time anyone reminded me of the difficult day ahead, I cried.

When that day actually arrived, I prayed that God would help me get through it. It seemed almost more difficult than the actual day that Bob died.

I just wanted to be alone, not even talking to anyone. Twice when the phone rang I ignored it. My recorder told me it was my son calling from California and my sister-in-law phoning from Kentucky, but I didn't want to talk to them.

As soon as the florist shop opened, I purchased a bouquet of silk flowers to put on Bob's grave. The red and white carnations reminded me of the flower spray that had been near his casket, with the banner "Loving Family" spread across it.

Bright August sunshine warmed the car as I parked near the white birch tree that was my landmark at the cemetery. A sprinkler spewed water in a controlled arc, making it difficult to escape the spray as I walked across the grass.

Crabgrass hugged the perimeter of the grave, and weeds encroached on the marker. The permanent metal vase implanted in front of the marker was totally obscured. I hadn't been back to the grave since early spring, and its lack of maintenance surprised me. The manager of the cemetery had assured me it would have "perpetual care," but I realized then the term included only lawn mowing, not clipping around individual graves.

I went home and returned to the cemetery with clippers, garden gloves, and a paper bag for weed deposit. By then the sprinkler had been moved to a different section.

As my clippers chewed away at the weeds assaulting the marker, I began to feel my depression lifting. In a strange way it was almost like doing a service for Bob. Since he had died on his birthday, I felt as if this was my birthday gift to him.

When I stood to survey the manicured marker, I felt relieved of sorrow and able to face my world. Through the healing balm of lawn clippers, God had granted me His peace and composure.

Each year that anniversary day is difficult for me. Grief is a wound that never heals completely, but always our Lord is there to help us through it.

Thank You for always being there
when I need Your comforting touch.

God enters by a private door
into every individual.
RALPH WALDO EMERSON

54

LATE ANSWERS

*Trust in the LORD with all your heart and lean
not on your own understanding; in all your ways
acknowledge him, and he will make
your paths straight.*
PROVERBS 3:5–6 NIV

After the loss of a loved one, we may want to scream at God and ask, "Why did You let this happen?" Parents who have lost a child may want to demand why his or her life was cut short. If our pastor dies, we may want to know why God took him home to heaven when he was working so hard to tell others about his Savior. If a spouse has died, the plea may be even more fervent. Why? Why? Why? It may take years to discover the answers to our "whys." Hindsight is 20/20, but then again, we may never know why some things have happened.

God does not give us the answers to all our questions (Deuteronomy 29:29). He is sovereign, and He knows what is best. He may take our loved ones to heaven, but He leaves us here for a reason. He asks us not to depend on our own understanding but to "acknowledge Him" and trust Him to direct our paths in ways we might never have thought possible.

Margaret Grant, whose evangelist husband died in open-heart surgery, now ministers alone to people of all ages, from preschoolers to Alzheimer patients. In her Christmas letter to me, she wrote, "I often wonder if

Willard had survived surgery, would I have been able to serve this way. I dare not question the Lord's reasons or plans. I simply rest on the leading of the One who has safely and carefully led me throughout my life."

Catherine Marshall felt devastated when her pastor husband died of a heart attack at an early age, but God used her writing to reach more people than he did. Her books sold over sixteen million copies, and these included several collections of her husband's sermons and prayers. She wrote her first book, *A Man Called Peter*, soon after his death. It was an autobiography of their life together. Not only was it a bestseller, but it was also made into a popular movie.

A friend lost her teenage son in an accident before she was a Christian and before I knew her. Since then I have often heard her say that God used the tragedy to bring her to Jesus. She clearly remembers the day she was washing her kitchen floor, after he died, and in the anguish of her deep grief she cried out to God. His peace flooded her soul and gave her a reassuring joy she had never known before. It completely changed her life. She turned the loss of her son into an outreach to other children, and through her work with Child Evangelism many youngsters have been brought into the Lord's fold.

As time passes, maybe God will give you the answers to the many "whys" you may have. If He doesn't, He can give you the faith to trust Him more.

Dear Lord, I do have questions, but I am
thankful I can trust You to direct my life.

Never think that God's delays
are God's denials.
Hold on; hold fast; hold out.
Patience is genius.
COMTE DE BUFFON

55

DARE TO DREAM

*Delight yourself in the LORD and he will
give you the desires of your heart.*
PSALM 37:4 NIV

John Millen wanted to study art. He yearned to do something creative, something more satisfying than making money and having the perks and prestige of his high-paying job as vice president of an insurance company. At age forty-six, with a wife and three children to support, the idea at first seemed crazy. But his passion for it continued, and with his wife's support he summoned the courage to do it.

It was not an irrational decision. He carefully planned his escape from the corporate pressure that demanded 120 percent of his time. He paid off his house, he enrolled in two art classes, and he launched his own public relations consulting business on the side to buffer his financial loss of income. Other executives privately expressed envy of his courage, and his resignation gave the company's photography coordinator the nerve to do likewise. At age forty-four Elizabeth Allen left her position in the corporate world to pursue a long-desired nursing career.

Mary Anna Robertson, born in 1860, was five years old when she first tried her hand at painting. That initial leap into the creative world of art cemented a desire that would stay with her the remainder of her life. She especially liked painting landscapes, using the juice of blueberries and elderberries to color her pictures.

Since she was one child in a family of ten children, her parents agreed she should leave home to earn her own living as a hired girl when she was twelve years old. When she was twenty-six and doing housework for a man with an invalid wife, she met a hired hand whom she married a year later. Farming and parenting then became her main focus in life, but Mary Anna never forgot the joy she found in painting.

She was almost eighty years old, however, before she began to paint in earnest. Her husband had died by then, and her hands had become stiffened by rheumatism. Today we know her as Grandma Moses, whose simple paintings of red barns and white houses, horse-drawn sleighs, cows, chickens, and children are loved the world over. And she never had any lessons in art.

What is the desire of your heart? Perhaps the loss of your loved one has given you more time now that you, too, could pursue an earlier ambition. Maybe it is just a simple desire, such as learning to play the piano or knowing how to quilt. Whatever it is, talk to our Lord about it, and with Him take the first step to accomplish it.

*Lord Jesus, thank You for
making me able to dream.*

~

*Only through experience of trial and suffering
can the soul be strengthened,
vision cleared, ambition inspired,
and success achieved.*
HELEN KELLER

56

FORCEFUL FAITH

This is the victory that has overcome the world,
even our faith.
1 JOHN 5:4 NIV

Hudson Taylor felt certain God was calling him to go to China as a missionary. At age twenty-one, after several years of study and preparation, he finally reached the shores of Shanghai, China, on March 1, 1854. When he arrived, however, he found that civil war had ravaged the country for four years, and his evangelism was given a cool reception. His eyes became inflamed and he suffered headaches. Forlorn, miserable, and homesick, he wrote long letters back to his parents and sister.

Discouragement battered him, but his faith persisted. John 14:13 became his favorite verse of scripture, and he claimed its promise several times each day: Jesus said, " 'And I will do whatever you ask in my name, so that the Son may bring glory to the Father' "(NIV). He developed the habit of rising early in the morning, lighting a candle, and spending time alone with God. Those who knew him sometimes said that before the sun rose in China, he was awake and worshiping his Lord Jesus Christ.

During his fifty-one years of service there, his forceful faith produced much fruit that did indeed bring glory to the Father. He founded the China Inland Mission, which established twenty mission stations, brought 849 missionaries to the field, and trained more than seven hundred Chinese workers. Entirely through prayer and faith, the mission raised four million dollars for the cause of Christ, and he developed a witnessing Chinese church of 125,000 members. It has been said that at least 35,000 were his own converts, and that he baptized some 50,000.

George Mueller had a similar forceful faith. Over a century ago in Bristol, England, he catered to the needs of more than ten thousand children in orphanages that he provided for them. For more than fifty years, he took complete care of them solely through the avenue of prayer.

Over Mueller's lifetime, he estimated he had received answers to more than fifty thousand specific prayer requests, and at least five thousand of them were granted the same day as his petitions. He maintained a notebook with his needs noted on one page and God's provisions recorded on the opposite page.

You may not feel God has called you to go to China or urged you to feed thousands of orphans, but your faith through Jesus Christ can move similar "mountains."

Dear Lord, please help me to have a "forceful faith." Help me to accomplish whatever it is You want me to do for Your glory.

~

Prayer is a cry of hope.
FRENCH PROVERB

57

A New Beginning

*You have granted him the desire of his heart and have
not withheld the request of his lips.*
Psalm 21:2 NIV

Stephen Push lost his wife in the terrorist attack of September 11, 2001. She was a passenger aboard American Airlines flight 77 when it crashed into the Pentagon. They had been married twenty-one years.

"My wife was the most important part of my life. She was my reason for living," Stephen said during an interview on the 6:30 evening news that commemorated the second anniversary of the 9/11 attack.

As a grieving husband, Stephen became an activist on Capitol Hill, proclaiming that our loved ones paid the ultimate price for the worst American intelligence failure since Pearl Harbor. Being an activist, however, did not completely fill his empty heart. Then one day while he was surfing the Internet, he met a woman on-line who was also acquainted with grief. Debra Lavalle lost her fiancé to a heart attack five months before 9/11.

Stephen and Debra started corresponding via cyberspace. When they finally met in person, it took only five hours of being together before he proposed to her. A week and a half before their interview on the evening news, they were married. The TV showed pictures of them in their festive attire beside their multitiered wedding cake.

"I like to think his wife and my fiancé put it all together in a better place," Debra quipped.

"I will always be changed by 9/11," Stephen said. "I will never be the same person, but I am happy again." Both he and Debra work now for Families of 9/11, an organization based in New York that helps those who lost loved ones in the attack.

The interviewer asked, "What do you tell those widows and widowers who still say, 'I can never date again. I will sleep alone the rest of my life'?"

"Everyone has to deal with grief in his own time and in his own way," Stephen replied. "But be open to the possibility of a change. Six months ago I thought I would be alone for the rest of my life."

Two years after 9/11, Stephen Push still grieves, but he no longer has to do it alone. Perhaps God has someone who will come into your life to help share your grief. He knows your needs and the innermost desires of your heart. You can trust Him with your future.

Dear Jesus, You know the deep "desire" of my heart. Please guide my future and help me to serve You, whether I do it alone or with someone else.

~

Matches are made in heaven.
ROBERT BURTON

58

TELLING OTHERS

"Go home to your family and tell them how much the Lord has done for you."
MARK 5:19 NIV

When Jesus and His disciples went across the Sea of Galilee to the region of the Gadarenes, they found a man with an evil spirit who had been living in the tombs (Mark 5:1–20). No one could control him. He was so wild he even tore apart restraining chains and broke off the irons people had put on his feet. Night and day he wandered among the tombs, crying out and cutting himself with stones.

Jesus asked the evil spirit, "What is your name?"

"My name is Legion, for we are many," the evil spirits replied. About two thousand pigs were feeding on a nearby hill, and the demons begged to be sent into the swine instead of being cast out of the area. Jesus granted their request. As soon as the demons left the man and entered the pigs, the entire herd rushed into the lake and was drowned.

When people came out from the town to see what had happened, they found the man who had been demon possessed sitting by Jesus, dressed and in his right mind. Later, as Jesus was getting into the boat to leave, the man begged to go with Him.

"No," Jesus told him. "Go home to your family and

tell them how much the Lord has done for you" (Mark 5:19 NIV).

Jesus gives that same command to us also: Tell your family what the Lord has done for you. Has God sustained you through this time of great sorrow? Have you felt His comfort in a special way, or have you experienced His answer to a prayer? Has He helped you handle a difficult situation or gone before you to open a necessary pathway? A shared blessing is one that is multiplied. It blesses the one who shares it and the one who hears it. And God gets the glory.

Children, especially, will remember how the Lord helped you handle a difficult situation. It will be a reservoir of help for them when they, too, are faced with difficult situations.

The mother of one of my friends couldn't sleep the night after her husband died. In the darkened room, the lighted numbers in a clock on her bedside stand noted the minutes as they slipped away. Finally she decided to count her blessings. One by one she recalled the ways her Savior had uplifted her. Before she dozed off, she had accrued three hundred blessings.

Maybe you, too, have had that many to relate to others.

Thank You, Jesus, for Your many blessings.

In blessing others, blest.
ALEXANDER POPE

59

MEMORY TRANSFER

*"We will. . .build a monument so that in the future,
when your children ask,
'What is this monument for?' you can tell them."*
JOSHUA 4:6–7 TLB

When the Israelites were ready to cross the Jordan River and go into the Promised Land, God held back the waters like a dam and allowed them to walk across on dry land. The priests carried the ark before them, then remained in the middle of the river and waited as all the people passed by.

Before the entourage started, God told Joshua to select twelve men, one from each tribe, for a special task. After everyone was safely across to the other side, the Lord gave further instructions. The men were to return to the middle of the river where the priests were still holding the ark, and each man was to carry out a large rock. They were to use the rocks to build a monument that would remind their children how God had held back the Jordan River when they crossed over to the Promised Land (Joshua 3:12–4:7).

Ensuring memories for our children—and future generations—constitutes a precious legacy. Recently at a Christian women's club meeting, one of the members told me about losing her grandmother.

"I loved her so much," she said, with tears moistening her eyes, "and I want so much for my children to know what a wonderful person she was."

"How old are your children?" I asked.

"Three and five. Each holiday I am going to write a keepsake letter to them and tell them how my grandmother observed that special day. For instance, on the Fourth of July she always produced homemade ice cream for her family, and at Christmas she and the kids always went with her husband to cut down a fir tree on their farm. Each holiday she always did something special like that."

"I think that is a beautiful idea," I told her. "I wish I had written down more details about my grandparents for future generations. Kids today don't know much about that 'horse and buggy' era."

Perhaps a memory book about your loved one would be a cherished gift for your children or grandchildren. Many bookstores have publications that could help you do this. They ask such questions as "What did you do on your first date? What do you remember most about your wedding?"

Memorials are important, whether they are about crossing rivers or eating homemade ice cream.

Father, thank You for memories.

*A life-long blessing for children is to fill them
with warm memories of times together.
Happy memories become treasures in the heart
to pull out on the tough days of adulthood.*
CHARLOTTE DAVIS KASL

60

FLYING LESSONS

*Now faith is being sure of what we hope for
and certain of what we do not see.*
1 PETER 5:7 NIV

W hen you step into the unknown, faith is knowing there will be something to stand on or you will be taught how to fly." This is a quote by Barbara J. Winter that was published in *Guideposts*. It describes so well the faith I needed to claim after my husband died. At age seventy, I sold the home I had lived in for forty years and negotiated to buy another one in a different city. This loomed as a frightening venture for me, and I prayed for the ability to "fly."

I waited a few years after losing my husband before I embraced this prospect. I had no family, just friends, around me, and I felt I should be near one of my two sons as I grew older. So I prayed about the decision and launched out to purchase a new home a half-mile from my younger son and his family. My sons live thousands of miles apart, and just choosing which one to live near was in itself a difficult decision. But God was helping me to learn how to "fly."

As I started to pursue all the preparations involved in the move, I began to have doubts about whether I was doing the right thing, or whether I was doing what the Lord wanted me to do. Then one morning when I was listening to a Christian radio station, God gave me the assurance I needed: " 'For I know the plans I have for you,' declares the LORD, 'plans to prosper you and not to harm you, plans to give you hope and a future'" (Jeremiah 29:11 NIV). Another "flying" lesson.

After the moving company loaded all my furniture and possessions onto their van and left, I was alone in the vacant house. My footsteps echoed as I walked from one room to another to check that everything had been taken, and to say good-bye. This was the house my husband and I had moved into soon after we were married. We brought home both sons to this house after they were born, and they had grown up in it until they left for college. Each room bulged with memories.

When I was finally ready to shut the door and lock it for the last time, I remembered the verse in Philippians that says, "But one thing I do: Forgetting what is behind and straining toward what is ahead" (Philippians 3:13 NIV). Life would never be the same again. But don't look back; enjoy the future Jesus has ready.

Maybe God has "flying" lessons for you also.

Dear Jesus, show me the future You have for me, and help me to learn how to "fly."

It is not what happens that matters,
but how you take it.
HANS SELYE

Scripture Index

Find more encouragement in these books from
Barbour Publishing

Drawn from bestselling books and authors,
these new compilations are perfect for anyone
needing a quick spiritual pick-me-up.

365 One-Minute Meditations
Come Away My Beloved
Frances J. Roberts
978-1-60260-053-9

365 One-Minute Meditations
God Calling
edited by A. J. Russell
978-1-60260-052-2

365 One-Minute Meditations
God Is in the Small Stuff
Bruce Bickel and Stan Jantz
978-1-60260-051-5

365 One-Minute Meditations
My Utmost for His Highest
Oswald Chambers
978-1-60260-050-8

Available wherever Christian books are sold.